Esoteric Encyclopedia of Eternal Knowledge

VERNON HOWARD

Four Star Books
128 S.W. I Street
Grants Pass, OR 97526-9913

Four Star Books

128 S.W. I Street
Grants Pass, OR 97526-9913

HOW THIS BOOK CREATES SELF-NEWNESS

This book contains a wide variety of guides and inspirations by which you can change your life in an astounding way. Esoteric teachings can uplift anyone just as swiftly as they are permitted to do their good work. They answer questions and banish problems which may have been burdens for many years. This book contains dozens of fascinating stories about men and women who found a new world.

Your own mind is the key which unlocks the secrets of life. In order to use your mind with full power, follow these guides:

1. Select any item in the *Esoteric Encyclopedia* and give its message your full attention and interest for a few days. Since each item is complete in itself, you will receive one outstanding message, plus several extra ones.

2. Keep a list of the items which speak to you in a special and personal way. In order to mine more gold from them, review their points regularly.

3. Join or form a study group to discuss and absorb these teachings. There is great power in a group of earnest men and women who want to know what life is really all about.

Just as the eager roots of a tree stretch out to find water, let your thoughts reach out to find, at last, true guidance and healing.

VERNON HOWARD

ACCEPT YOUR HARMONY

The classic song 'The Lost Chord', is a summary of man's ceaseless search for something beyond himself. Written by Sir Arthur Sullivan and Adelaide Proctor, the song tells of an organist who played idly upon the organ keys. In a weary mood, he was unaware of what he was playing, until by chance he struck one grand chord of inspiring harmony. That one magnificent chord quieted all sorrow, answered all questions.

The organist sought once more to experience that divine combination of notes, but it eluded him. But he remained hopeful that sometime, somewhere, he would find and hear it again.

Within every human being are all the needed notes with which to play the grand music of True Life. We need only eliminate false notes and invite true ones in order to hear the harmonious music sleeping within us.

At this very moment you can accept your life-harmony. Accept it.

ACCOMPLISHMENTS

A teacher said to his audience, 'We have been studying together for six months. By this time our intended accomplishments should be clear. Please give them to me in single sentences.' The students responded:

'We are seeing that esoteric principles are the very essence of a whole and sane mind.'

'We are passing beyond the limits of our present nature.'

'We intend to change what happens to us by replacing unconscious behaviour with conscious action.'

'We are aware of how we have confined our own minds, and so now intend to give them room to roam.'

'We seek to make the inner government supreme.'

'We wish to see quite deeply that chatter about social reform is just an evasion of personal transformation.'

'We are making ourselves willing to take what the truth has to offer.'

ACTIONS TOWARDS OTHERS

You can sweep aside all arguments and questions concerning your actions towards others with one simple rule. Any action that is *truly* right for you is truly right for another. And what is truly wrong for you is also harmful to your neighbour. You are not separate from your neighbour except on the physical level. By this rule it is not only unhelpful to practise man-made moralities towards others but downright damaging, for they increase the illusion that the artificial is the real. Put it another way. Any action of yours that fails to develop your own inner strength is useless to others. If a lighthouse is to help passing ships, its own light must radiate into the fog.

When hearing this, a learner asked, 'What do you mean by man-made moralities?'

'Anything pretending to be good while having cunning self-interest behind it. Examples are all around you.'

ADMISSION TO REALITY

A person attending a truth-lecture for the first time usually feels that everything he hears is against him. That is simply because he still protects the very chains he wishes so desperately to drop. However, he cannot as yet see this contradiction in himself. He is unaware of how he clings to the very source of his misery. For example, when with others, he insists upon conforming to the popular opinion of how he *should* behave. The real man is not present at all. He fights fiercely to retain his stage role because he knows no other way to act before others. The thought of being caught without memorized words and movements is so terrifying he instantly rejects everything which seems to threaten him.

Suppose a person in this predicament possesses one small but definite wish to become real. What will help him? He can run out of places to which to run. At first this appears even more agonizing than the forced stage role to which he runs constantly, but he finally glimpses something. He sees how abandonment of the costume pays for admission to the real man inside.

AFFECTION FOR ROYAL PRINCIPLES

We have attitudes towards everything. We may be aware of how we think and feel towards members of the family or towards politics. But how rarely do people ask, 'What is my attitude towards royal principles?' A story from history will help here.

Many years ago a group of archaeologists were excavating the ruins of the famous and ancient city of Pompeii. Some French soldiers, who were quartered in the area, were assigned as assistants in the digging. But the work of the soldiers turned out to be unsatisfactory. They were too careless and awkward in handling the delicate objects which were uncovered. They were replaced by more competent workmen.

We must not handle the truth carelessly. It deserves our honour and affection. More and more, as understanding expands, do we handle it with gentle care. And in wonder we see that the affection and gentleness have come from a higher place.

AGILE MIND

The absorption of these teachings creates an amazingly agile mind. No longer tied to hardened habits, it leaps like a skilled athlete from one situation to the next, handling all with ease. Having no self-centredness, such a mind wastes no time and energy wondering how a situation might be hurtful or beneficial. Having no interference from anxious thoughts, it simply acts. When meeting a troubled person it acts wisely by not falling under the influence of the other person's gloom. When needing a new chair it simply buys a chair it can afford without regretfully wishing it could afford a better chair. When confronted by a new challenge it walks right into it and out again, unharmed, for it knows that harm comes only by fearing the challenge.

Anyone can test all this for himself. He will then see that the great proof and only proof is self-proof. Whoever tastes an apple for himself will never need to ask others about its flavour.

ANGUISH
Mr and Mrs E. came early in order to ask a question before class began. Mr E. summarized his question, 'May we hear more about the nature of mental anguish? How can it be ended?'

'Anguish is nothing more than a mental movie which the sufferer carelessly permits to run through his mind. Where there is no mental movie there can be no anguish. Experiment with this. The next time you suffer, make a deliberate attempt to break the horror film in your mind. Even if succeeding for one second you will see that anguish ends when the film ends. The horror has no existence except in the imaginative film. You can aid your own experiment by ceasing to have a hypnotic fascination for the horror film. To summarize, repeatedly break the unreeling mental movie, then see what a different person you become.'

ANOTHER WAY
Many years ago a temple of higher knowledge was being built on a hill overlooking the Nile. The man who would become its chief teacher wanted a suitable proverb to be inscribed over the front door. He thought about it many times as the work progressed. The morning finally came when the foreman needed to have the selected proverb, so he asked the teacher for it. 'Please come back in an hour,' requested the teacher, 'I will then have it for you.'

While thinking about it, the teacher wandered near a skilled workman who was gently correcting the work of a young man. The teacher heard the older man make the encouraging remark, 'There is another way.'

Over the years as troubled students and visitors entered the temple, their first lesson was inscribed over the door. It read: THERE IS ANOTHER WAY.

ANSWERS ABOUT PROGRESS

'I am not advancing as swiftly as preferred. How can I understand more quickly?'

'You can understand as much as you are willing to understand. If progress is slow, examine your willingness.'

'You say we must not become dependent upon a teacher. How can this be avoided?'

'It is good and necessary to hear an esoteric fact from someone who knows, but go on from there until hearing it from yourself.'

'How can we estimate our actual level of understanding?'

'The true test of a man's spirituality is his ability or inability to remain content when nothing exciting is happening.'

'It would help if I clearly knew my goal. Who am I trying to be?'

'The person everyone wants to be is a person who is not in trouble with himself. You can succeed.'

APPLY THESE TEACHINGS

'What is man like? What is the actual nature of society? What am I like?' Search for the answers to these questions until you find them.

Man is a contradiction. He is like the rope in a surging tug of war between two brawny teams. The strained rope moves first in one direction, then in the opposite direction. It is caught, taut, unable to free itself from slow torture. This is seen clearly in the idea of authority. One part of a man wants to find and worship an authority, someone who tells him what to do, who relieves the need for independent thinking.

But another part rebels instinctively against giving his mind over to another human being.

Those who apply esoteric teachings to their lives can end the strain of self-contradiction.

APPROACH SELF-HEALING

Do not postpone self-healing. Approach it now. When physically hungry you do not delay your steps towards the dinner table. So why postpone the psychological satisfaction you could have right now? When reaching the spiritual table, dinner is already there, waiting for you. Act with the assurance of this, then you will see how true it is each time. Even when trembling with apprehension that it might not be there, go ahead anyway. Approach *while* trembling. Dare to do what timid parts of you do not want to do. After a while you will be fearless, bold, and always satisfied.

What confirms all this? There is only one confirmation and it is all you need. You confirm from yourself through a totally different kind of feeling about yourself and your life here on earth. It is a feeling you had not known before, completely unique. You *know* it is right.

APPROVAL FROM OTHERS

Someone commented, 'All of us feel trapped by the very social system we have created.'

'Would you like to know why you feel this way?'

'Yes, please.'

'Because you are so tensely concerned with what others think of you. Have you ever noticed this in yourself? That is your trap. You want to appear happy and successful and confident before others. Pull out of the trap. Have no need for such appearances. These are false desires by which you hope to feel secure, but they are the very cause of insecurity. Make a choice. Which do you want — approval from others or your own life?'

Who owns you? A domineering person? Someone you fear may one day leave you?

What owns you? Nervous haste? A compulsive desire to

win over another person?

Own yourself.

AROUSE YOURSELF

Picture a man who cannot keep a straight course down the pavement because the wind keeps blowing his hat away. That is how fear interferes with right and progressive living. A frightened mind cannot possibly work for the true interests of its owner. Insight into one fundamental fact enables us to get on with our true business. Fear exists because we carelessly permit psychological winds to lead us away. We do not know our own power for self-command. Man rarely inquires, 'Is all this frantic chasing really necessary?'

It is not necessary.

There is one thing you must never tolerate. You must never tolerate the conclusion that your life must remain the way it is now. It need not remain this way at all. Arouse yourself and exclaim, *'It is time to explain myself — let us stand up.'* (Walt Whitman)

ARRIVAL OF PERSONAL GOODNESS

How does authentic personal goodness arrive? Not by performing exterior actions considered good by society, for society prefers appearances over facts, words over realities. Goodness arrives simply by using our minds correctly, which means to never take ideas about goodness for goodness itself. A mind stuffed with ideas about goodness does not create a good man any more than placing sugar in a cup changes the nature of that cup.

Look at it. The idea 'good man' is simply an idea, and man is not merely an idea. He is a Wholeness which includes ideas. You do not call a wheel the whole automobile; you do not refer to an arm as the entire body. So the test of goodness is to see whether *all* of the man is good. What if he preaches goodness but secretly scorns people? What if he feels good when giving a gift but does so in order to appear generous?

True goodness belongs to the Whole. Any man or woman within that Whole is truly good.

ARTIFICIAL HAPPINESS

There was once a man who was terribly unhappy, but had trouble admitting it. His pressure drove him to consult a man of real wisdom. Instantly sensing the situation, the wise man asked, 'What is the foundation of your happiness?'

'I have a fine family,' the visitor explained, 'plus considerable wealth and a dozen exciting involvements. That is the foundation of my happiness.'

The wise man nodded. 'I have another question.'

'Yes?'

'How happy does your happiness make you?'

Happiness having a human foundation is artificial. As human conditions change, the so-called happiness sinks with them. True happiness has no dependencies, also it seeks nothing. The sun does not seek to be the sun. It just is.

ASK THE QUESTION

Many people hesitate to ask certain questions about life for fear there may not be an answer, or that the answer will be frightening. Have nothing to do with this attitude. Ask the question you fear to ask. An honest question attracts an honest answer. Never mind if the answer seems contrary to what you now believe, for surprise at what you hear is part of your healthy climb.

Nancy said during an evening class, 'You urge us to ask short and direct questions. I feel timid about asking such a blunt question, but will do it anyway.' Nancy paused a moment, then asked, 'Can I really find the way out?'

'Of course you can. The reason you can find the way out is because it actually exists. Man is like a prisoner in a cell who weeps and wails over his unhappy location, but never examines the door of his cell. He fails to realize that the door is really unlocked. Prove your liberty for yourself. Push on the door. You are out!'

ASTONISHING DISCOVERY

A prospector climbed a mountain to seek gold. On the way up he fell down and struck his head. In his dizziness he imagined he had found hundreds of gold nuggets. So wandering around town, he offered non-existent gold to everyone he met. He was completely unaware of what he was doing.

A few days later he fell down once more, but this blow cleared his head. In shock and dismay he realized his former folly. 'How incredible of me to imagine I possessed gold,' he told himself.

Then an astonishing thing happened. Once realizing he did not possess gold he began to find gold nuggets.

Spiritual riches follow awareness of poverty. That is the one and only order of things.

Anyone can see the difference between real and imaginary inner riches. He can inquire, 'Do I feel rich when all by myself, or do I constantly need others to reassure me?'

ATTACHMENT AND FREEDOM

Said Arthur, 'A friend of mine was highly enthusiastic about an organization he had joined which was going to make everyone happier, including himself. For several weeks he could hardly talk about anything else. He could hardly wait to attend the meetings where everyone excitedly planned the great crusade which would save the world. Then, abruptly, he dropped the whole thing, losing all interest. In my curiosity I asked him what had happened, but he resented my questions. I would like to know how a man could turn from hot to cold so suddenly. Please explain his behaviour.'

'Why are you so surprised at typical human conduct? Insecure people are for ever attaching themselves to this or that group in a frantic attempt to escape the inner terror. But since it is only a stage performance, the curtain must fall. Such people are quite sure they know what they are doing, only to be dipped into doubt by the next person to whom they speak. Then they are off to a new theatre. There is only one solution. Learn what it means to think from your own mind, then think from it.'

ATTENTION

Several men and women applied for admission to an esoteric school. Asked the teacher, 'What do you think I need from you?' Some applicants suggested money and service, while others thought the teacher needed respect and loyalty.

'What is deeply needed,' explained the teacher, 'is your faithful attention.'

Remember the power of *attention*. Give persistent attention to a problem in spelling and you soon correct it. Likewise, attend to arising thoughts and moods. By noticing worry you can proceed to the next step of realizing it has no power over a conscious mind. Alert attention to a negative state enables you to refuse to be taken over by its peculiar and harmful fascination. Incorrect attention is like a man at a football match who watches the *referee*! Remember the power of attention — and remember to use it.

ATTRACTIVE REASONS

People who misunderstand ask, 'Why should I study esoteric science?' That is like asking, 'Why should I drink water?' Everyone should study this superior science because:

It attracts satisfying rewards.
The old ways can only repeat old problems.
No task is more fascinating.
Self-oneness is our supreme goal.
Esoteric science has workable answers.
It makes you skilled and efficient.
Frustration is no fun.
Human relations become successful.
Painful decisions will cease to arise.
It is the one sure way out of self-bondage.
Life is meaningless without it.
Its invitation is both gentle and strong.
Contentment is better than insecurity.
It opens a new world before you.

AUDIENCE AND REACTION

Picture a large audience fortunate enough to hear a talk by an awakened man. How will the average audience react when hearing his honest message? It can be analysed.

Many will be sincerely confused. There is real hope for them if they refuse to permit conditioned thought to judge what they hear. Their original nature can then explain and clarify.

Some will be there as silent arguers. They use the familiar trick of hoping to feel right by proving the speaker wrong. They suffer from themselves.

Others, though disturbed by the message, sense its honesty and rightness. One bar in their self-imprisonment has already melted by their first glimpse of the difference between trueness and falsehood.

A large number whose vanity feels threatened by the facts will have a hostile reaction. In most cases their habitual stage roles of being peaceful people will conceal the hostility.

Some, on the edge of a breakthrough, will respond with a mixture of inspiration and doubt. They are in a good position but must nourish the seed of truth with more receptivity.

AUTHENTIC GIVING

Esoteric education is drastically different from ordinary schooling in many ways. However, in one way they are similar. The completion of one course qualifies you for the next. The following paragraph contains an example of this.

After you have made some progress you may meet someone who is interested in the esoteric way but who knows little about it. Remember the doubts and timidities of such a person. He is unsure of his new mental environment, like a stranger in a distant land. You can help him or her by reviewing your own early experiences. Tell him how puzzled you were at first, but how the clouds of doubt steadily faded away. Urge him to read, discuss, experiment, in order to see esoteric riches for himself, just as you did. By assisting earnest people you assist yourself. By this kind of authentic giving you receive something you never had before. This is one operation of esoteric law.

AUTHENTIC STRENGTH

The French philosopher, Rene Descartes, speaks of his first rule while searching for truth: *'The first was never to accept anything for true which I did not clearly know to be such.'* Epictetus, the ancient Roman philosopher, adds: *'Relying on what? Not on reputation nor on wealth nor on the power of the law, but on his own strength ... for these are the only things which make men free.'*

From the clear viewpoint of esotericism, authentic strength consists of several inner states, including:

Living from natural essence.

Absence of artificial personality.

Thinking for oneself.

A fondness for what is right.

Absence of illusions and superstitions.

Understanding of one's mind.

AVAILABLE SUPPLY

Some of the regions along the Persian Gulf are among the driest on earth. There are no streams and rain seldom falls. Human life would be impossible in some of these areas except for a fortunate occurrence. One day some swimmers dived deep enough into the sea to make a startling and delightful discovery. Undersea springs poured huge quantities of fresh water upwards towards the surface.

The swimmers obtained goatskin bags, dived through the layer of salt water and filled their bags with pure water. The life-giving water became available to all who knew the secret of the undersea springs.

A courageous plunge into our inner world will also reveal delightful discoveries.

AVOIDANCE OF DISAPPOINTMENT

Randolph asked, 'How can I avoid disappointment at not getting what I want?'

'Understand how life really works. That is the one way and the great way to end the pain of not getting everything attractive to your eyes. Think of persons or objects which you once valued, but which you now ignore. That is perfect evidence that their value existed in your state of mind, not in themselves. You may not believe that this applies to your present desires, but it does. Save yourself time and trouble by learning all about the actual workings of life.'

'You mean I can actually change the way I see life?'

'Change the way you see yourself and you change the way you see life. Change the way you see life and the life is new. When you are new, so is your life, for they are exactly the same thing.'

BAFFLING CONDITIONS

Take a condition which baffles you. It can be about future plans, despondency, finances, anything at all. You may believe yourself incapable of finding an answer, or may assume there is no solution at all. Drop these beliefs. Ask a question about the puzzling condition, then listen for the answer from your true nature. The self-dialogue might go like this:

'How can I solve this condition?'
'By understanding it.'
'How can I understand it?'
'By ceasing to fear it.'
'How is that accomplished?'
'By refusing to give it false power over you.'
'Why do I give it false power?'
'Because you do not as yet realize your actual supremacy.'
'Then I need only seek more self-knowledge?'
'Yes, for you are the answer as well as the question.'

BANISH LABORIOUS THINKING

Mere intellectual consent to rightness is not enough. The intellect is only part of our cosmic nature, and it takes the whole man to be a right man. Wholeness is rightness itself. It is easy to mentally and verbally agree with a statement such as, 'Each man must rescue himself.' But few people act as if they believe it. Most men and women want to make their own problems while expecting others to unmake them. Intellectual consent to rightness is like standing at a window to welcome a visitor but not opening the door to let him in.

Only an active welcome counts.

When really understanding something we no longer need to think about it. A competent cook just cooks. We strain at thinking only in the absence of comprehension. A student-cook has to search for answers and decisions. Notice this for yourself. The aim of esotericism is to show men and women how to understand with the whole mind, thus freeing them from laborious thinking.

BARRIERS TO OVERCOME

Lack of self-dependence holds us back. We cannot be like the man standing outdoors who asked his friend whether it was raining. We must see for ourselves.

Discouragement must be given no room. The reason we can succeed is because our unknown strengths are greater than our known weaknesses.

To be easily influenced is a barrier. A free mind is neither influenced nor injured by newspaper headlines, a cruel face, abruptly changed plans, a loss, threatening society.

Action is blocked by carelessly taking publicly promoted delusions as realities. The truth is what it *is*, not what millions of people *think* it is.

Words and labels seem to create obstacles, but they are powerless. Withdraw the labels from personal conditions and you are free, so withdraw labels such as 'unliked' and 'desperate'.

BASIC INFORMATION

Every man wants to be different from his neighbours. He wants to be richer or more pampered or handsomer or more popular. Yet everything he does to attain these aims makes him commonplace, for his neighbours are doing the very same things. The world is composed of duplicate machines having mechanical beliefs of being individualistic.

A man becomes different by doing something his neighbour rarely thinks of doing. He becomes unique by plunging straight into his haunted psychic system with a determination to clear out the ghosts.

Are we defeated or disgraced? That should be the very signal for redoubling our efforts to locate the den of defeat and disgrace. They hide only in a wrongly-operating mind which still pursues superiority over others and so fears to end up disgracefully inferior.

When our terms are the same terms as truth, we meet everything in life on our own terms. We do so without even thinking about superiority or inferiority towards others, for they do not exist in truth.

BATTLEGROUND OF OPINIONS

A man once wanted some opinions so he went to the market place where opinions were sold. Opinions were so plentiful they were also cheap, so he bought and took home hundreds of them.

The man then met every day with friends to exchange opinions. They always ended up quarrelling and hurting each other, each man insisting that his opinion was the right one. But strangely, they continued to meet and to quarrel, for they felt an odd pleasure in the fiery exchange of hostility.

But one evening, after an angry meeting, this particular man sensed the self-damage in this kind of childish behaviour. So he went to a wise man who said, 'Every acquired opinion has an opposite opinion. Men live by these opinions which in their delusion they call facts. Fighting is inevitable. Toss out your opinions. I will then tell you about the Single Fact, which has no opposite, and which is sometimes called God.'

BE AUDACIOUS

Never wait for good things to come your way. That is the anxious method of most people. Notice the nervousness in waiting. 'Will it really come? How long must I wait? What if it fails to arrive?' There is nothing good in all that.

To wait for something means we are living within a wrong view of time. In turn, this means we are not living within the completion of the present moment. Happiness does not involve time. There are no clocks in the cosmic sky.

You do not ask for enough, not nearly enough. Timidity

wins nothing. Ask for more and receive more. Asking Truth to solve some petty problem is like asking Michelangelo to paint your front door. Why don't you ask Truth to solve all problems by revealing and ending their inner causes?

Why settle for less? Be audacious.

BEGIN LIFE ANEW

Suppose you ask someone, 'If you could start life all over again today, what would you do different?' He would not stop talking for a week! Yet that man will do the same things today that he did yesterday and never give them a second thought. He dully repeats his blunders because he believes there is no alternative. There is, but he must see what he does not see at present. Chained to time, he does not sight his freedom to start life over again every day, every second. He thinks life is a mechanical clock which measures time. It is not. Real life is a timeless renewal in the present moment. We are within that moment.

Commented a student, 'We have studied the topic of time over many months, and I see its importance. For example, I see how the wrong use of memory provides the illusion of time. But something still eludes me. How can we deeply realize the non-existence of time? Stated differently, how can we see that right now is all the time there is?'

'Try to live in some other time than right now.'

BE HOME TO YOURSELF

Man's unconscious carelessness with his own life is similar to a small boy playing with a toy train. As long as the boy operates the right switches the train speeds normally round the track. But distracted by the shout of a friend outdoors, the boy rushes out, leaving the train unattended. Returning a few minutes later to find the engine and cars in a wreck, he shouts, 'How did that happen?' He is either unable or unwilling to connect himself — his absence and inattention — with the wreck of his valued train.

'Be present and be attentive!' That is what the great avatars of the ages have been trying to teach to tearful mankind. 'Connect what happens to you with the fact that you are not where you should be – in your own mental home. Be aware of society's lures and distractions. See how misfortune occurs because the mind thoughtlessly rushes out to play a new game at the slightest invitation. Stay at home with yourself.'

BE INTERESTED

Have you ever considered the power of simply being interested in something? Do so. When interested in travelling to a holiday area, your interest carries you there. When interested in buying a new car, you are impelled by your interest to obtain one. The interest you have in cosmic exploration is wonderfully healthy and naturally exciting. Give it full permission to grow, which it will do. That is like giving yourself permission to be happy.

Baruch Spinoza, the Dutch philosopher, was interested. He developed his practical teachings while living in seclusion in various parts of Holland. Offered a high position at the University of Heidelberg, he declined, preferring private study to public prominence. That is the rare and independent spirit which succeeds.

BENEFICIAL SUBJECTS

Let a group discussion or personal meditation revolve around these meaningful subjects:

Self-adventure is cause for self-cheer.
Turn knowledge of truth into living truth.
Examine motives carefully.
Be absolutely fearless towards everything.
Live by the laws of your own nature.
Blend casually with change.
Be not the slave of admirers.
Never assume you already have the answers.
Allow yourself to face disturbing facts.
Do not remain apart from yourself.
Look until you see.
Learn the secret of active inaction.

Only the individual can build individuality.
Self-awakening is true help for others.
Your future is as free as you are.

BEST TEACHER

A young man desired to find the true way. Applying at an esoteric school, he was accepted. With great hope and enthusiasm he began his first day of training.

At the end of the week his beautiful dream had faded. He brought his complaint to one of the teachers. 'I came here for spiritual instruction,' he stated, 'but was put to work cooking dinners and delivering messages. I wish to grow more swiftly, so may I not give full time to private meditation and classroom discussion?'

The teacher patiently explained to the young man what he had explained over the years to many other young men. 'Your mind still works in divisions. You wrongly assume it is more spiritual to be in the classroom than the kitchen. You falsely believe more is gained by carrying a book than carrying a message. Do not divide life like that. You are with your own mind every moment, so be in school all the time, regardless of physical surroundings. Your mind is your best teacher.'

From that day forward, the student advanced swiftly.

BETRAYAL

Earl spoke up in a class in California, 'Several of us were discussing the topic of betrayal, and would like more light.'

'What is called betrayal or treachery can occur only when self-betrayal is also present. By self-betrayal I mean a careless ignorance of one's own mind. It means one has not exposed certain illusions which make him gullible to others. For instance, a person who gets hurt in his relations with the opposite sex must see several facts. He must see where his intense desire for the other person closes his eyes to the other person's self-serving schemes.'

'So we must attend to our own inner state,' commented Earl.

'In the absence of self-betrayal, no one can betray you. If you know a panther when you see one, do you play around with it?'

BEYOND THE WHIRLPOOL

Running away from a crisis is not the same as running towards reality. A clear realization of this assists us to perform the magical feat of using troubles to end troubles.

A distressed person is like a man in a boat caught in a whirlpool. He rows desperately away from the centre of the whirlpool. When reaching its edge he obtains a certain relief and sets down his oars to rest — which is his careless mistake. He is still in the whirlpool, so sooner or later its mechanical forces will draw him back into the swirling centre. The crisis will end when he refuses temporary comfort in favour of permanent freedom. This is won by continuing to row until passing over the line dividing the edge of the whirlpool from the free waters beyond.

Connect these facts with any kind of crisis, perhaps that of a broken human relationship. Notice how people are more eager to relieve their distress than to wisely examine and end its cause. Make up your mind to row beyond temporary comfort to lasting liberty.

BLUNT FACTS

Said a teacher to his class, 'Part of your work is to face the forthright facts about human nature. Please supply some blunt facts.' The class responded:

'The masses of humanity live in mechanical moralities which change overnight at the sight of supposed advantages.'

'If you want to know where you are living from damaging self-images, notice where you are most easily offended.'

'A change in exterior circumstances does not change a man's spiritual level, for a pygmy on a mountaintop is still a pygmy.'

'No one is more unbearably egotistical than a stupid man who has had good fortune.'

'If your relationship with another person is based on his

neurosis, that relationship is in trouble.'

'When a foolish man says he wants your advice, he really means he wants to hear the same silly advice he would give you.'

BODY AND MIND

A teacher of ancient India was watching his students practise archery. As one archer drew his bow and lined up the target, the teacher stepped forward and instructed, 'Look at the clouds.' After obeying, the student heard a second command, 'Gaze at the woods.' The student looked towards the nearby forest. Nodding, the teacher finally instructed, 'Now look at the target.'

The students knew what was happening, for their teacher often interrupted daily activities with unexpected lessons.

Said the teacher to everyone, 'Realize what you should *not* do. When wishing to hit a target you do not gaze at clouds and woods. I have just taught your physical body a lesson, for it needs spiritual training as well as mind and emotion. You will now command your body a bit more than before. For example, it will sit more at ease during a lecture; it will not restlessly wish to be out playing games. Along with mind and emotion it will look in the right direction and so hit the spiritual target.'

BOOK OF TRUTH

A good and wise king wished to teach his young son to live and rule righteously. One day he gave the boy a book of spiritual instruction, entitled *Book of Truth*.

'This is the most valuable book we possess,' said the king. 'Come with me to the library. You will see what I mean.'

In the library, the king nodded towards the filled shelves. 'The books are arranged according to their value to mankind. Those on lower shelves speak to us about agriculture, the seas, and other topics for practical living. The higher the book the greater its value for us. Please notice the topmost shelf, which is at present empty. This high place is reserved for the book you now hold. Please place it up there, while never forgetting where it belongs. You see,' said the king with a sad shake of his head, 'some people who use our national libraries are careless. They place lower-level topics above this supreme book. Always give this guide the lofty position it deserves.'

Over the following years, the son equalled his father's wisdom by keeping the *Book of Truth* in its rightful place.

BOULDERS AND LESSONS

Ernest opened the group discussion by saying, 'Today at work I experienced an example of a mistake we make. I was working with another man in clearing some boulders out of a field. The rocks were hidden by tall grass, so we could not drive round without risking a collision. Searching on foot we found and removed all the boulders from the field — so we believed. We drove only a short distance when the car bumped into a boulder we assumed was not there. Fortunately, there was no damage.'

Ernest looked at the others. 'See the lesson? We have been studying it for several weeks. When failing to see a negative trait we automatically assume it is not part of us. Then when bumping into the rock of reality we complain! We must remove the tall grass of our illusions and look at what is there.'

Peggy commented, 'It is strange how a human being will bump and injure himself for years and never ask why it happens. It is because we don't want to admit our part in the collision.'

BRIGHT EXPLORATIONS

When a honeybee finds a rewarding field of flowers he hastens back to the hive in great excitement. By performing an enthusiastic dance he informs his friends of the discovery. Because the flowers are real, his enthusiasm is legitimate.

It is legitimate for anyone to be highly enthusiastic over esoteric discoveries. All discoverers are.

Associate freely and frequently with esoteric facts. But remember that association is not penetration. Let them sink into your psychic system to perform their healing. Let them succeed in their purpose. This answers all questions about the mind, including, 'Where am I thinking incorrectly? What must I learn? How can I recognize an exciting but self-defeating idea? What is the nature of new thinking?' The answers lift the load in a way which no man can imagine.

Reflect upon what you know and you have a comfortable yard in which to rest. Reflect upon what you do not know and you have a bright world to explore.

BUILD COURAGE

'I am conquered by worried emotions. How can I begin a campaign to regain self-command?'

'See emotions as surges of energy. At their original source within you these energies are not negative, but pure and powerful. Realization of this fact will gradually channel energies towards self-command.'

'You say we must see what we are really like. This seems like a mysterious task.'

'It is easy to solve. Everything that happens to you in the exterior is telling you about the interior. See your inner world as the author of your outer world. You are like whatever you receive from the outer world, for the inner and outer are the same.'

'Speaking generally, what do awakened men try to show to stubborn men and women?'

'A man clings to his cherished illusions, like a child afraid to let go of his favourite but broken toy. He must be shown it is broken, which will build courage to let go.'

BUILD PERSONAL EFFICIENCY

We must learn to perform everyday tasks with maximum ease and efficiency. This is part of esoteric schooling. There is a definite relationship between one's level of cosmic insight and one's competence in conducting business or managing a home. Cosmic growth naturally expands our talent in such areas. Take the talent for giving careful and sustained attention to a particular task. A mind that has found itself gives wholehearted attention to an enterprise. Not distracted by psychic imps, it sees everything clearly and settles everything instantly.

As an exercise in all-around development, select a small activity and give it your whole and sustained attention. See how long you can stay with it. Watch for and guard against both inner and outer distractions which try to tug you away. If pulled away, return at once.

Using daily tasks like this expands psychic powers which then turn around to give a helping hand in daily tasks.

CAPABLE COMMAND

To illustrate the lesson of the day, a teacher told the following story:

'The captain of a holiday ship was skilfully directing the voyage when a storm suddenly struck. The ship lurched, knocking the captain against a pole, making him dizzy. In his unclear state of mind he forgot that he was the capable captain of the ship. Wandering dazedly along the deck he asked various passengers for help in directing the cruise. Since the passengers knew nothing of navigation, they either gave him foolish advice or stood there in frightened silence.'

The story concluded, 'After a while the captain regained full use of his mind. Realizing his captaincy, he resumed his capable command.'

Realize your life-captaincy.

CAREFREE DAYS

In a group in London, someone asked about a carefree life. The inquirer concluded, 'Every daily step is taken in trembling caution. We are crushed by carefulness.'

'You don't have to be careful at all. Obviously we are not talking about carefulness when crossing a busy street. That is instinctive caution which perpetuates the human race. I am speaking of scheming carefulness which tries to hide pretences. This is a terrible way to spend the day. Hide nothing, protect nothing, and you are as carefree as a sparrow in the sky. This is beauty in action. You don't have to take thought about yourself, for there is no artificial self screaming for protection. You walk in and out of any human situation as you please, having nothing to win or lose. This is because you have won the Invisible Prize.'

CATEGORIES OF KNOWLEDGE

Knowledge can be divided into two categories. There is Everyday Knowledge and there is Cosmic Knowledge. Everyday Knowledge consists of facts useful in daily affairs, such as knowledge of mathematics or foreign languages or of the weather. Cosmic Knowledge consists of a deep insight into the how and why of the universe as a whole. A person possessing Cosmic Knowledge knows the cause of and the cure for human sorrow. He also knows how few really want to obtain these rescuing facts.

A person can have considerable Everyday Knowledge, while having no Cosmic Knowledge — though fully believing he is a spiritual authority. All he really possesses is a sackful of *man-made ideas about spirituality*. Or, a person — the rare person — can have considerable Cosmic Knowledge, plus enough Everyday Knowledge for handling daily affairs.

Learn the difference between the two. And remember, you can obtain Cosmic Knowledge only from someone who really has it.

CAUSE AND EFFECT

Seeing the causes of our effects is essential. Start with this basic rule: Cause and effect occupy the same place. Cause is not in another person's rude behaviour towards you, with the disturbing effect being inside you. Both cause and effect are within the person feeling the disturbance. The individual's *response* contains both cause and effect. Blaming another for our distress is like blaming the postman for not bringing any letters. Delivery starts in another place.

A conversation with Roger clarifies this:

'Why am I always doing things I really don't want to do, such as agreeing to participate in social crusades?'

'Because wrong causes drag you there, such as a wish to gain feelings of self-worth. It will never work; it is a bottomless bucket. You don't need to feel self-worth. You need to drop the illusion that you need a feeling of self-worth.'

CAUSE OF TENSION

Tension is caused by opposing desires. An individual may desire to get involved with social and community activities. He hopes to gain public prominence, which in turn may offer financial advantages. Or he gains a self-flattering image of being a generous contributor of his intelligence and knowledge.

But by psychological law, these desires must be opposed by another set of wishes. Many times when called upon to serve he would rather stay at home and watch television or go out and play golf.

Tension results. He is painfully trapped between opposing desires. He is like a desperate man stranded on a lonely island who thrills at the sight of approaching ships — until he sees their pirates.

Only an understanding of vanity-pleasing desire can end his tension. He could start by seeing that he is not really caught between demanding people and his own private wishes. He is trapped only by his own misunderstanding of what he needs for a contented life.

CELESTIAL CITY

A group of unhappy men and women heard about a peaceful place called Celestial City. Wishing to live in it, they consulted a wise man who told them, 'Go to the edge of town. There you will see footprints. Follow them all the way to the Celestial City.'

When locating the footprints, part of the group turned back immediately, complaining, 'But they lead straight into the frightening wilderness.'

The rest of the group followed the footprints for a short distance, but several more stopped when it started to rain.

After a few more miles the group broke up into two quarreling factions, each demanding the right to lead the expedition. The battle raged so fiercely they forgot all about Celestial City and returned home to continue the fight.

When observing all this, the wise man explained to his disciples, 'Because of man's dazed mind, this is what always happens. Still, people must be told about the footprints. Every once in a while a persevering man or woman follows them all the way to Celestial City.'

CHALLENGING SENTENCE

There was a teacher who understood the imperfections of those attending his classes for the first time. Many came with smug and unconscious assumptions of already knowing the truth, while others found false pleasure in arguing and denying. The patient teacher had developed an effective method for helping newcomers pass beyond their wasteful attitudes. It consisted of forcing them to frankly question the very lives they now lived. He did this by writing a single sentence on the blackboard, after which he asked the pupils to ponder it silently for ten minutes. The sentence read:

This way of life you protect so fiercely and fearfully — honestly, now, what has it given you in return?

Later, some of the students told the teacher how they had responded to the sentence:

'It made me think.'
'I needed its jolt.'
'It made me more honest.'
'I saw its valuable lesson.'

CHANGE

Kenneth requested, 'Please discuss change. It is often so unexpected and unwanted it shakes our so-called security.'

'Look at change from a totally new viewpoint. You have no self which is apart from the All, and this All includes change. Therefore, being one with the All, you are also one with change. Now from that viewpoint, peer deeply into change. Changes take place in our age or in human relations. How does that affect your real nature? In no way. Allness is merely adding variety to the way it expresses itself. Now look even deeper. You cannot be hurt because you yourself are not apart from the change, for you are change itself. And listen to this. Since *you* are the All, *you* allow change, *you* approve it, *you* are happy with it.'

Kenneth gasped, 'That is enough to think about for a month!'

CLEAR VISION

Every event presented to you by life is pure in itself. It appears distorted only when personalized thought leaps in to declare 'I like' or 'I dislike.' In this condition we do not see the event as it is, but according to our experiences and acquired preferences. Two men can look at the same woman with opposite reactions. One of them, hoping to meet her, sees a charming girl before him. The other man, who has been hurt by her, looks bitterly at a deceitful woman whose surface charm can drop like a brick. Not seeing her impersonally, both men are slaves to their own reactions. The first man is enslaved by impulsive desire, while the other man is chained by resentment.

A conscious man sees everything with unclouded vision. This is possible because mental clarity contains no self-reference. The false self is absent, leaving only pure perception. A conscious man is aware of human deceit, but is unharmed by it because his psychic system resides on a higher level than the deceit.

We can live under events or above them, depending upon our cosmic level.

COLLAPSING WORLD

Take a look at what you call your world. Notice how much strain and effort it takes to keep it in place. Repair the west side and it breaks down on the east. What an endless and futile battle.

The next time your world begins to fall apart, stand calmly aside and let it fall as far and as fast as it wishes. Offer no resistance. Fight nothing. Just stand there as a calm and impartial observer.

Have no fear in permitting this. There is nothing to fear. Not at all. It only appears that way for a while.

Ask yourself why you should fight the collapse of what you call your world. There is no reason whatever — no real reason.

So let your world collapse swiftly. With a bit of good fortune it will collapse even more swiftly tomorrow. Then, with complete collapse, out of the ruins will arise a new world.

COLOURFUL RIVERS

Many rivers throughout the world are named after their colours. Among them we have the Orange River in South Africa and the Yellow River in China. The United States has a Red River, Green River, White River. The Rio Tinto, in Spain, passes through several colours, including red, purple, green.

The colours come from the nature of the terrain through which the rivers pass. The presence of coloured soil in river bed and shrubbery on river bank determines the appearance of the flowing waters. Or, the very absence of particular colours decides their appearance.

But surrounding colours are not obstacles. Regardless of appearances, the rivers flow freely through deserts and around mountains to reach their natural destinations.

Likewise, personal circumstances do not become obstacles when we permit our original nature to flow freely, as nature intends.

COMMON OBJECTION

Said Norman, 'As a beginner, there are many things I do not understand. Here is one of them. If we give up feelings of excitement over winning wordly successes, won't life become dull? Won't we live as motionless and meaningless vegetables?'

'That is a very common objection made by beginners. Let me ask, Norman, have you reached the other shore as yet?'

'No, sir.'

'Then how can you describe its nature? Why do you call it dull? Can you accurately describe something you have not seen? No. Do not confuse assumptions with facts. You fear the other shore, for it requires you to give up false feelings of life. False feelings of life consist of exciting emotions which seem to tell you who you are – that you are a sufferer, a dynamic businessman, and so on. Strangely, beginners fear the loss of their very misery, for misery seems to confirm their identities. As for dullness and meaninglessness, they do not see that this is the precise condition now punishing them.'

COMPETITION

Many strange and wonderful events happen along the true path. One of them is the gradual disappearance of a sense of competition. You no longer feel yourself to be in a tense contest which you hope to win but fear you may lose. This relaxation falls upon every area of life, including the way you earn your living and your human relations. What delivers this victory? The ending of the false sense of self, which is always trying frantically to win someone or gain something. This ending is your new beginning. Though participating in human affairs, you no longer need to compete or to win, for you have already won – but in a new way which others will not understand. You will never go back to your old way.

Just as a bird-watcher follows doves and owls throughout the woods in order to learn all about them, follow these ideas with an intense interest.

CONSCIOUSNESS DELIVERS FREEDOM

Everyone is born in this world under certain mechanical laws of life. For example, negative attitudes are mechanical. When one man is cruel to another man, the offended person seeks revenge. Both behave mechanically and both are punished by their ignorance. This is the present state of humanity. The evidence is all around us.

We are set free from mechanical laws by rising above them. Transcendence comes through understanding their nature.

Consciousness is not mechanicalness, therefore, only consciousness and awareness possess liberating insight into mechanical movements. So become highly conscious of the following laws:

Your thinking determines your life.

Your actual nature creates your future.

Your attitudes attract your experiences.

Your aims decide your destinations.

Let your thinking, your nature, your attitudes and aims be conscious, not mechanical. See how everything changes.

CONTROL OF LIFE

For a man to win control of his life he must first lose the illusion of already having control. This requires steadfast self-examination, for everyone has a pocket of resistance which never wants to admit lack of control. A man or woman may even publicly confess to an uncommanded life, but secret vanities persist in their claim of having personal power. We fear that a total admission might make other people think less of us, or that we might think less of ourselves.

Our self-examination must reach the point where we are willing to let go of the pretence of having control over particular habits or life in general. We may do it timidly at first, but we finally let go because we now see it as right action and the only action possible.

By seeing that we cannot do anything, doing becomes possible, but it is not our personal power. It is Cosmic Action.

CORRECTING MISTAKES

There is only one way to correct mistakes, but it works perfectly when understood. All mistakes occur because we live only with the mechanical part of the mind instead of with the whole mind. Take a person who gets into endless trouble by doing and saying wrong things. This is his way of life. Why? Because the mechanical part of his mind — to which he clings stubbornly — cannot see anything above its own level. He is like a foolish civilian who insists upon wandering around a battlefield, then complains that soldiers are shooting at him. The mechanical-minded man never sees himself as the cause of his punishment, never sees the source of tension within himself.

Mistakes are corrected by transcending mechanical thoughts and rising to a full use of the total mind. The whole mind knows a mistake when it sees one, and wants nothing to do with it.

CORRECTION OF MISUNDERSTANDING

Maxine requested, 'Please correct a misunderstanding we may not even know about.'

'No friend or stranger has ever caused you mental or emotional pain. No one has power to hurt you. Then what happens? You hurt yourself through wrong reactions. You feel bad over an insult? What gets insulted? A demand on your part that others should respect you. Why do you have this demand? Because you want so-called respect to confirm your false notions about who you are. Why do you have these illusory notions? Because you still think you possess a separate ego, a distinct identity apart from the Whole. Why do you continue in this painful error? Because you do not take time to see the facts. Take time.'

COSMIC FLIGHT

A student of higher thought said to a friend in the class, 'I am becoming increasingly aware of the need to change myself inwardly. I have seen how the inner cause produces the outer effect. It was surprising at first, but I now realize how each of us makes his life whatever it is. Seeing this, I also see how other people find it difficult to grasp, for I was once in the same mental fog. I have a relative who is always trying to improve his life by making exterior changes, for example, by moving from one city to another. He comes and goes the same bewildered man. But I'm sure you know all about this mistake. All of us make it.'

'Right,' replied the friend. 'If an aeroplane's motor is faulty you can't make it fly by giving it a fresh coat of paint.

All of us have to really see this fact, then our very perception becomes a power for cosmic flight.'

COSMIC LAWS

A teacher said to an advanced student, 'Please give the class a fundamental fact about cosmic laws.'

'Cosmic laws are here to help, not hinder.'

Whether we call them cosmic laws or psychological principles or spiritual rules, their study returns profit. Here is one for beneficial examination: Each man has the same attitude towards himself that he has towards others. This is absolute cosmic law. It means a person acts with either the same kindness or the same harshness towards himself as he acts towards others. An attitude within a man is never divided; it is a single attitude which either nourishes both himself and the other person, or subtracts from both himself and the other man. Play pleasant music for yourself and you play it for everyone else around you.

COSMIC SANITY

To gain more knowledge for yourself, you must give what you have already received. An aeroplane pilot can raise himself to a higher altitude only by also raising his passengers. This does not necessarily mean to become a teacher; it means to naturally radiate whatever truth you have acquired. This radiation is as effortless as sun rays.

The only gift we have for the world, and the only worthwhile gift, is a portion of Cosmic Sanity. If we have replaced stubborn self-will with Cosmic Sanity, it will be sensed and received by all who want the gift.

Not all want the gift. But some do. You will know them. They will know you. You have something in common in which there is no sense of competition. You may talk about it, but at other times you will look at each other with silent understanding.

COUNTERFEIT CONFIDENCE

Counterfeit confidence, with its always dependable dips into dejection, is cured by a clear recognition of its artificiality. So put it under a mental microscope. Look closely and see that false confidence always depends upon something in the exterior. It might be a comfortable home life or many friends or a promising future. So counterfeit confidence is in fear of losing its seeming security to unexpected change. So it is not confidence at all, but merely a bulge of thoughts and feelings. Like a balloon, the greater its size the larger its emptiness.

Deeper examination reveals the arrogance in counterfeit confidence, which easily turns towards violence. Its negative nature has a compulsive need to expand itself, so it has no conscience towards those who get hurt by its explosions.

It is the whole man who has real confidence. As a project, think about this. Get assistance from other sections in this book which discuss self-wholeness.

CREATIVE ENERGY

Begin today to use this remarkable procedure: First, become clearly aware of every arising feeling of pressure or discomfort or nervousness. Just notice how they persistently rise up and take over mind and body. Next, become conscious of the great energy possessed by these ruthless invaders, for they do indeed move with great force.

With all this in mind, proceed to the next important phase. Think of this energy as being totally pure in its original form. Do not see it as pressure or nervousness which must take you over, but as a force under your own command. This is the way it can be. It is like a raging river tamed by strong banks.

Finally, think what can be done with all this power! See how you can help yourself by releasing it towards positive goals, including personal poise and clear judgment. Let yourself be both inspired and renewed.

CREATIVE WRITING

Take paper and pencil and write down a single word, almost any word. Starting with that word, build a single, clear and informative sentence. You might write, 'The integrity of my mind is all that matters,' or, 'True courage is the willingness to hear facts which go contrary to my present beliefs.' Find other examples throughout this book.

Practise this from time to time. It expands creative thinking. It builds logic and insight. Here are several good words for starting the sentences.

Progress
Awareness
Learn
Remember
People
Knowledge

CURE OF SUFFERING

Anyone can save himself years of heartache by studying and applying the following facts.

Suffering is caused by: Unnecessary separation from our original nature. A fearful wish to escape sorrow instead of facing and understanding it. Blaming other people and circumstances for our unhappy state. Lack of guiding knowledge about anguish. Refusal of self-reliance and self-responsibility. Living in imaginary happiness. Following false prophets and useless teachings. Clinging to the habitual instead of to the true. A general wrong use of the mind.

Suffering is cured by: Examining the nature of suffering with a scientific mind. Refusing false comfort from people who use your heartache for their own benefits. Floating on the fact that you can be your own doctor. Not resenting or fighting a sorrowful condition. Abandoning secret pleasure in feeling troubled and persecuted. Using your whole and unified mind. Getting so weary of suffering you resolve to no longer go along with it. Understanding the general cosmic laws of life.

DAILY GUIDES
Observe the kind of advice you are giving yourself, then decide whether you like the results of that advice.

Anyone wishing to make it on his own must first discover what is really his own and what is not.

There are great possibilities for anyone who asks after getting his feelings hurt, 'Why am I such a slave to others?'

Something exciting is happening inwardly when you no longer look forward to something exciting.

Fear of ridicule can be overcome by always being who you really are.

You can use your thoughts correctly or you can let them use you incorrectly.

Make it your aim to no longer let artificial personality speak and act in your name.

An inability to understand an esoteric fact contains a favourable element, for it means that at last we are trying to open the right door.

DAILY PRACTICE
Once a fact has been mentally absorbed, find ways to practise it in daily contacts. When fact meets experience, understanding explodes.

Raymond had the following fact in his mind: 'The very same pressure a man puts on another, knowingly or unconsciously, is the very same pressure with which he squeezes himself.' Raymond agreed that this was psychic law, but it was not as yet liberating understanding.

One day Raymond was about to put pressure on a store clerk whose carelessness had caused considerable inconvenience. Observing himself, Raymond saw how he was agitated by the very pressure he was about to apply. Instantly, he dropped the impulse — *and at that moment he understood the path to freedom.*

Go and do likewise.

DAYDREAMS

Take something which is difficult to accept or understand, then make an effort to see what it means. That, really, is what turns on the light.

Take daydreams. Daydreaming may be the easy way out, but they make the return trip an unnecessary ordeal. We are better off staying at home in the first place. Daydreaming fails to take total life into consideration, thus creating division. It is like believing that Mona Lisa's smile is the whole picture. A man imagines himself as a great lover or dashing adventurer. That is his daydream. Success as a lover or adventurer cannot quiet his fear of the unknown future. That is his division and conflict.

A mind operating wholly has no need to daydream. It has no need to go anywhere in a frantic attempt to find itself. It already has.

DAZED MANKIND

A news story told of a motorist whose car ran off a cliff and tumbled into a canyon. Not seriously injured, he stumbled away from the car to seek help. But his dizzy mind sent him in the wrong direction, away from the highway. His battered car was finally sighted by passing motorists, who called the police. The dazed man, who believed he was heading towards help, was found wandering in some wooded hills, two miles from the highway.

Man's dazed mind functions wrongly. Correction could come swiftly were it not for a particularly faulty part. He is unaware of his actual condition. He takes darkness for light, chooses the artificial over the real. So like the motorist, he is in an incredible position. There is nothing more incredible than a person being uninvolved with his own rescue while believing he is helping himself. That is the startling condition of those who wander in the wrong direction, those who mistake society's sly propaganda for authentic guidance. Those wishing self-rescue must get involved with something higher than society's confusion.

DELIGHTFUL PROGRESS

We must remind ourselves every day of the delight of what we are doing in this cosmic world. This is no sorrowful way; this is the way out of sorrow. Even when our aims seem out of reach it is no reason for dismay. Our very pressures can be turned into delightful progress, just as storming steam drives a ship. Emotional agitation makes us forget the true way? Let every agitation be the very signal for remembering the true way. Someone hurts or disappoints us? Let us immediately cut loose from the false power of hurt and disappointment.

You can rescue yourself. You have everything you need for succeeding. This is a fact, regardless of how heavily the world seems to press down upon you. Here is one way to proceed. When upset by anything, not knowing which way to turn, ask yourself, 'How can I think towards this condition with my own original mind?' That is a highly intelligent question. It leads to the answer you need.

DELIVERANCE FROM LONELINESS

Everything wandering man needs to possess can be given to him simply and directly. There is no problem of supply. What every individual needs is instantly available. Then what is the difficulty? It can be stated plainly. It is the individual's refusal to listen. He anxiously refuses to acknowledge the existence of anything above his present thoughts and acts. In this book we are learning to listen. That is enough. What we permit ourselves to hear will do the rest.

Anyone can permit himself to hear at this very moment the message which delivers him from loneliness. First of all, we must see where loneliness exists — the only place it exists.

Loneliness resides in that part of a man's mind which wrongly declares that he possesses a self which is apart from the Universal Whole. He does not in fact possess such a separate self. He is within the harmony of the Universal Whole. This is not starry philosophy. This is practical fact. Reflect upon it. Connect it with everything else you have learned. Watch what happens to feelings of loneliness.

DEVELOP SELF-DEPENDENCE
Give yourself a small task every day to make your mind work better in common experiences. To climb mountains, first reach hilltops.

A good start is the development of self-dependence. Many areas of life require assistance, as when determining the quality of a new car. But declining assistance in other areas builds self-reliance.

Take an occasion when you cannot locate an article lost around the home. Do not take the easy way out. Resist the impulse to call for help from wife or husband. Force your mind to rely upon itself only. Make yourself think of additional places where the article might be hidden. Simple exercises like this quickly awaken sleeping resources, which soon invade and conquer new worlds.

DIALOGUE
The following dialogue took place as Carl read out his three questions in class:

'Why do most human beings fail to hear the facts of life?'

'Because you can rarely talk to the human being. You talk to the successful businessman or the busy mother or some other unconscious self-label. The label has no interest in hearing anything outside of itself.'

'The idea of spiritual rewards puzzles me. I know they are totally different from worldly benefits, but I need an explanation. What is a spiritual reward?'

'The reward of not being self-divided is to not be self-divided.'

'You speak of the need to catch our first glimpse of

another way. How can we catch this first glimpse?'

'Think deeply about the absence of ego-competition. Think what it means to not be in ego-competition with other people. That can lead to a first glimpse of another way.'

DIAMONDS EVERY DAY

To be engaged in self-discovery is the one activity which makes life truly fascinating. It is like finding diamonds every day. Whatever excitement we get today from false goals must be paid for tomorrow. But to increasingly discover the extent of our natural freedom is to receive endless payment.

Self-liberation is a full-time business. You can practise it any time you like at home or office. No time on earth is better spent. Be wholeheartedly receptive to the following fact: The first principle of profitable self-work is a persistent and honest and non-judgmental observation of everything you think and say and do.

If in the dim light you cannot make out a mountain trail you are hiking along, your one wish is for more light. More light. That is what self-exploration is all about.

DIFFERENT PSYCHOLOGIES

Esoteric psychology is to ordinary psychology like the Mississippi River is to a shallow country stream. Ordinary psychology teaches adjustment and compromise instead of self-exploration, change of scenery instead of change of nature.

For one thing, esotericism is not deceived by the well-rehearsed stage performances in which people try to appear wise and understanding. It knows all about human masks. Here is an example of its perfect insight:

When, on very rare occasions, two awakened men meet, they instantly and fully understand each other.

When, less rarely, an awakened man meets a hypnotized man, something else happens. The awakened man understands the hypnotized person, but the hypnotized man has no insight into the enlightened individual.

When two hypnotized men meet, which happens millions

of times a day, neither understands the other, and so they fight and suffer.

DISCOVER NEW TALENTS

A class of beginners said to their teacher, 'It has been said that man employs but a fraction of his natural talents. How can we find and use them for loftier living?'

The teacher placed a covered object on the table, then instructed a student, 'Feel the object under this cloth and tell us about it.'

After following instructions the student responded, 'It feels like a bell.'

Removing the cover the teacher said, 'It is indeed a bell. Look at it and give us more details.'

'It is about eight inches high and made of brass.'

'Ring the bell and tell us more about it.'

After shaking the bell the student said, 'Its tone is clear and musical.'

The teacher nodded. 'Each time you examined the bell with a new sense you discovered another characteristic. You did not limit your understanding by limiting your use of natural powers. So it is with man. He possesses many more cosmic talents than he ever employs. Only by suspecting their existence within himself can he begin to use them for self-elevation.'

DISSATISFACTION

It is necessary to be dissatisfied with one's life if one is to change it. The self-complacent man, drugged with wordly success or with private daydreams, can never be different. His artificial satisfaction is surrounded by fear of loss, causing tension and irritability.

So we must be dissatisfied. That comes first. Then comes a crucial point. *Everything depends upon what we do with this dissatisfaction.* We can go wrong or we can go up. Great watchfulness is needed to turn dissatisfaction into elevation. It is a wrong move to bitterly blame others for our woes, or to escape into dangerous distractions, such as alcohol or agitating activities. It is wrong to assume that our usual ways of thinking have creative power, for ordinary thought changes nothing.

The right move is to sit quietly and do absolutely nothing about your dissatisfaction. Do not fight it. Remain with a quiet mind and spirit.

DISTORTION OF TRUTH

Beginners on the esoteric path always make the same objections and ask the same questions. Here is a typical dialogue:

'Esotericism says we must look within and attend to our own state of mental health. But this seems selfish and unloving. The great teachers, such as Christ and Buddha, taught that we must never think of ourselves, but must lose our lives in loving service to others.'

'They taught nothing of the sort. That is a cunning distortion of truth by the false self which wants to keep people enslaved. Christ and Buddha, who were truly enlightened, taught honest self-facing, not tricky self-evasion. You change what you are only by first seeing what you actually are. You go beyond yourself only through self-knowledge, which requires courageous self-facing. You can give pure water to another human being only if you first possess pure water.'

DISTURBANCE

There is an interesting difference in reactions when hearing false doctrines and when hearing esoteric facts. People are thrilled by a false teaching because in one subtle way or another it appeals to vanity. Deception has power only with the co-operation of unawakened people. But the hearer must now become the victim of depression, for the incoming tide must also flow out.

But the hearing of a true teaching awakens an entirely different response. To the hearer's surprise and dismay, he feels not inspiration, but disturbance. This is because noble truth is performing its honest task of exposing illusions masquerading as realities. But this disturbance is the seed of inspiration, an inspiration which will never flow away.

With this in mind, welcome any disturbance you feel when told the truth. Do not be afraid of being disturbed; just remain with that state. Disturbance is the doorway through which you walk beyond all disturbance.

DO NOT BE AFRAID

A teacher entered the classroom to declare, 'Whatever is unnatural is unnecessary. Fear is unnatural and therefore unnecessary.' The teacher uncovered a blackboard to reveal the day's lesson, then instructed, 'Review this list in silence for the next ten minutes, after which we will discuss it.' The students studied the list which read:

Do not be afraid:
To have no idea of who you are.
Of past or future.
To seek truth all by yourself.
Of having no excitement in your day.
To be completely wrong.
Of not getting attention.
To refuse to compromise with error.
Of your negative characteristics.
To keep going after a fall.
Of what people think of you.

DO SOMETHING FOR YOURSELF

One of the most terrifying periods of a man's life is shortly after he has won what he wanted. His success might consist of financial gain or domestic pleasure or anything else. It is during this sunset of a success that the thrill exhausts itself, forcing acknowledgement of the impermanence of thrills. With dread, he realizes what he must now do. He must wearily climb another and another desired mountain, falling off every new one.

But this is a clue. Every man who has ceased to fall off mountains has observed this repetitiously painful pattern in himself. After years of worried wondering what it was all about, he saw the answer. He was trying to do something totally unnecessary — prove himself. The realization dawned that self-proving is an endless road with thousands of sudden bumps.

Then came the courage to do something for himself for the first time in his life. Instead of trying to make illusions look like facts, he let facts end his aching illusions.

DOUBLE DECEPTION

Two students were discussing their search for a teacher. Said one, 'For years I sought someone who could help me. I met and left the self-deceived, the greedy, the dynamic parrots, those with a compulsion to teach, and many more false guides. But I finally found a man who lived the integrity he taught. But what about you?'

'I had an equally difficult time,' said the other man. 'I roamed from teacher to teacher, despairing of ever finding the right one. But I finally did. Then I spoke right up and told him he was the finest teacher I had ever met.'

'When did you tell him that?'

'Right after he told me I was the finest pupil he had ever met.'

DOUBT AND CERTAINTY

Self-doubt is one of the concealed pains endured by men and women. Like all mysteries, it can be solved through diligent investigation. Self-knowledge replaces self-doubt with self-certainty.

'Just how does doubt disappear?' asked one inquirer.

'At the start of our search we must think about these lessons, but must then proceed to the higher level of feeling them with our whole nature. Feeling provides recognition and certainty. A story illustrates this. A tailor of ancient Persia was also a teacher of esoteric lessons. Since his disciples lived in different cities, and were often unknown to each other, he devised a method of recognition in case they should meet. He gave each disciple a coat made of special material. Those owning a coat would know how it felt, so a quick touch provided instant recognition. When you learn to feel the truth, there is no doubt about it.'

DWELL IN LIBERTY

A man once lived in a country having many strict and oppressive laws. Along with the other citizens he was compelled to live in an unpleasant environment, and was forced to work at dreary tasks. His mind was heavy with sorrow.

However, with intelligent planning, he succeeded in escaping to a new country. But strangely, his unhappiness remained, for he thought, 'I am still a slave to cruel laws. I will be just as dejected as before.'

But everything suddenly brightened, for he was soon told, 'Banish your belief in oppressive laws, for here there are none. This is indeed a new country. In this land of true liberty you are free to live as you wish.'

There are no laws which compel anyone to be defeated and discouraged. A new nature dwells in liberty, so return to this nature and experience this liberty.

EASE AND ACCURACY

A deep-sea diver once explored an ancient Spanish ship which had sunk off the coast of Florida. He brought up a strangely shaped object covered thickly with the coral of centuries. When the coral was removed the object revealed itself to be a sundial. When set outside, the sundial perfectly resumed its work of telling the time.

That illustrates our task. By removing everything foreign and useless to our true nature, we perform as easily and as accurately as we were intended to perform. We can clean away the useless notion that life is against us, for the person who is one with himself is also one with everything else. By seeing this we can then banish feelings of being at the mercy of people and events, for our real nature has no such feelings.

ECONOMY

Built within everyone is a natural desire for economy. We do not like to waste anything, whether it is food or time or energy. The greater one's psychological health the more this natural inclination is followed. A healthy man knows that his economy is not selfishness. Wastefulness indicates failure to perceive what is truly valuable, like a hungry man who throws away the bread and tries to eat its wrapper.

Great benefits appear through living fully within this inborn sense of economy. One of them is the recovery of ourselves from those who drain us. Have you ever felt drained by talkative people? Ponder it. Sometimes we even feel it is kindly or necessary to place ourselves at the disposal of others. No. This violates the rule, 'Save yourself before trying to save others.'

Your wish for economy is trying to tell you something. Listen.

EFFECTIVE READING

Use these seven guides to profitable reading:

Read with an enthusiastic wish to discover what you and your life are all about.

Do not be discouraged if you do not understand various ideas at first. You will be helped by your deeper nature which does understand.

Read regularly. Use spare moments at office or at home to absorb a few principles.

Allow the truth to tell its own story. Do not permit stubborn thoughts to distort the story.

Read with a quiet, relaxed, yet alert mind.

Write down ideas which impress you in particular. Review and reflect upon these inspiring thoughts.

Remember, your purpose in reading an esoteric book is to enable you to read yourself.

EFFORTLESS ACTION

When really seeing something, when actually understanding, your behaviour changes towards whatever you see. It is effortless change, requiring no uncertain decision on your part. The appearance of Reality is itself the change, with you in oneness with it. It is like a boat floating downstream, either left or right in unison with the natural course of the river.

You have had times when you did not know how to proceed, as when considering a change of employment. Every tug in one direction was countered by a tug in the opposite direction. The solution is to see that your real nature can never be elated or depressed by either course taken, for it is superior to all results in human affairs. In that supreme perception, your everyday judgment is released to handle either course with perfect command.

EMPEROR OF THE UNIVERSE

Offer to make an awakened man the Emperor of the Universe and he will smile gently at the offer. He is already the Emperor of the Universe by not being separated from it by delusions. He does not know himself apart from the universe, any more than a particular cloud sees itself apart from the sky.

There is a great opportunity for the individual who willingly relinquishes the kind of individuality he now claims.

The entire secret of true happiness is to cease to defend yourself to the point where there is no longer anyone there to defend. Read this over several times. Connect it with everything else you have read. Think deeply about its meaning.

If it sometimes seems as if much is asked of you, remember a principal point. Everything asked of you is for your good — your true good.

ENCOURAGEMENT

Everyone who wants to get out of the jungle will sooner or later reach a certain stage in the journey. By learning about it now, you will be your own guide and own encouragement when reaching it. It is the stage where you can go neither forwards nor backwards. Too clearly do you see the folly of past ways, so you can never go back. At the same time you have no idea of how to push through the fog towards clear air.

This is quite normal. It is a usual stage in the jungle trail which is passed safely by all who escape the jungle. The terrible tension of self-contradiction is left behind at last, releasing natural energies to do constructive work.

Along with this comes a new feeling of relaxation, plus a profound understanding. You now see how dark forces tried to make you feel guilty over leaving false doctrines. You see how you were disabled by a fear of leaving the familiar but miserable. And now you are on your way, glad you stuck with it until winning.

END OF FRUSTRATION

A mind operating in its own recovered light is amazingly sharp. It sees what ordinary minds only imagine they see.

It sees that the clearness of the solution will be to the same degree as the clearness of the problem. Any attempt to find a solution without seeing the problem — the real problem — must fail. The real problem is confused human beings who insist they are clear. Seeking a solution without seeing the problem is like playing a ball game without the ball. Connect these ideas with the next paragraph.

No man is really frustrated by what happens to him. Frustration arises from feelings of helplessness, from dimly realizing he is not the conquering hero who can twist results to his liking. So his frustration is simply an exposure of his pretence of having an individual ego which can perform and succeed.

With the vanishing of the illusion of an individual self, frustration cannot occur, for then there is no one to oppose whatever happens. This is the state of union with the All.

ENDURING ESSENCE

A scientist was making a series of experiments with vegetable seeds. His aim was to produce larger and tastier harvests. While at work one morning he became aware of the absence of one of his highly prized seeds. He searched the laboratory thoroughly, but the seed remained mysteriously missing.

A few years later, when cleaning his car, he saw a seed in a dark corner, under the front seat. He recognized it instantly as the lost seed, for it bore an identification mark. He assumed the seed had somehow been carried to the car in his clothing, after which it had fallen below the seat.

When bringing the seed back to the laboratory, the scientist thought of all the places he had driven his car, thus exposing the seed to sudden changes from heat to cold. He wondered whether the seed still retained its essence of life within.

He planted the seed. It proved its endurance and hardiness by energetic growth.

No one should feel dismayed if something seems to be missing. It can be found.

ENLIGHTENED OBSERVER
There was once a man who found himself involved in one stormy experience after another. Whatever he touched turned into trouble, including marriage and financial affairs. He lived, of course, in deep distress. He tried to conceal this from others as best he could, for he wanted to be known as a man of poise and confidence.

His perplexity was colossal. He could never figure out why people spent most of their time planning ways to persecute him. He growled bitterly, 'My intentions are innocent and my manners are cordial — but look how I get kicked around.'

One day the man was cursing cruel fate when an awakened man observed him. The enlightened man spoke silently to the complainer. 'Sir, if you only knew what I know about you. But I can tell you nothing, for you would flare up in hatred. You secretly love the stormy experiences you claim to dislike. That is why you attract them. You are like a man who deliberately crawls into a wolf's den and then screams persecution by the wolves. You would rather feel like a persecuted man than feel nothing. Only when understanding all this will you cease to attract your own misery.'

ERASE WRONG BELIEFS
An Arabian legend tells about a stranger who set out loaves of bread on the northern part of a town. Everyone collected the bread while singing the praises of the absent stranger. He was absent because he was busy plundering the southern part of town.

Esotericism urges us to not be so distracted by apparent good fortune that we fall victim to our own carelessness.

If you want to reach London, forget Paris. If you want to reach a new place in yourself, forget everything unrelated to this aim. Take a look and see what can be done. Maybe you should forget physical action in favour of mental movement. Perhaps you should ignore most of the advice given you by people who want something from you. Maybe you should erase the belief that security resides in social involvement.

Take the direct route to yourself.

ESOTERIC EDUCATION

The capacity for growth into a new kind of person exists within everyone, just as a seed contains everything necessary to create a flower. So begin your esoteric education with lighthearted feelings of liberty.

When you were a child in school you were told what to study and how to proceed. A system of rewards and punishments was employed to keep you attentive. You had to obey or suffer the consequences.

But now you are an adult. You are no longer under school rules. Threats of punishment no longer exist. You can study what you like and ignore what you wish. You need fear no one. You need not be terrified of failure. No one can do anything against you.

Live according to these facts. Live as if you are out of school. Now you can begin your esoteric education, which is totally different. You graduate every day.

ESOTERIC PSYCHOLOGY

Said George, 'For thousands of years we have had the principles of psychology and philosophy and religion. We are no better off than before. Why?'

'No one wins inner victory by learning the principles of ordinary psychology. A donkey in a library is still a donkey. The accumulation of facts cannot by itself change anything. Only by investigating thoroughly a certain principle of esoteric psychology can a man become a new man. An individual must shockingly see how he lives from imaginary ideas about himself, then give them up. That is the whole story. A man should start with this fundamental plan, after which he can acquire right knowledge for assisting abandonment of his synthetic self. Remember, you want the facts themselves, not the labels which have been pasted on to a particular system of thought. Take the fact that we must listen to truth without the interference of collected opinions. That was a fact long before the labels of psychology and philosophy were invented.'

EVERYTHING CHANGES

As we walk the path, everything changes before our eyes. The facts which we may now take as enemies become our best friends, while the ideas which we now think are good and true will be seen as destructive and false. What we used to assume was a castle becomes a dungeon, while what we called a dungeon becomes our castle. Our values change in a way we cannot imagine. Our world is new because we are new.

We then realize that worry is an unnatural state which naturalness conquers.

We then understand what it means to be loyal to one's fundamental nature.

We then see wonders which have extremely practical benefits.

We then know for sure that inner light has total power over all false claims of darkness.

EXAMINATION OF THOUGHTS

A teacher addressed his students. 'Did you examine the food you ate today?'

'Yes, sir,' the students replied.

'Did you examine the purchases you made today?'

'Yes, sir.'

'Did you examine the thoughts you thought today?'

'No, sir.'

'Why did you omit the most important examination?'

Beginners sometimes wonder why they should bother to examine their thoughts. How strange. No one wonders why he should examine the kind of clothes he wears. We wear heavy or light clothing because our physical self is related to the weather. Wrong clothing makes us hot or cold. We should examine our passing thoughts because they are related to the social climate. Our thinking determines our poise or our nervousness out there. Our thoughts decide how others will treat us, decide our choices and the pleasant or unpleasant results of those choices.

Thought-examination expels wrong thoughts, leaving only those which harmonize perfectly with the exterior world.

EXAMPLES FOR GROUP DISCUSSION
As a class project, have volunteers supply examples related to the following list. For instance, an example of a right attitude is to see an irritable person simply as someone who still suffers from himself. Find examples of:

A right attitude.
Correctly used energy.
Rejecting self-defeating behaviour.
Overcoming spiritual timidity.
Seeing a truth for the first time.
Loyalty to celestial science.
Getting out of one's own way.
Independent thinking.
Dropping the useless for the valuable.
Flowing with self-harmony.
A progressive action.
Listening with a receptive mind.

EXCELLENT REQUEST
When seekers come to a real teacher they usually do not know what to say. Unsure of themselves they often compose a conversation with small comments and questions. An excellent opening is to request, 'Please tell us what we need to know.' A teacher might well respond with the information contained in the next three paragraphs.

Learn to follow events. That is what we always do anyway, though few realize it. Just follow whatever happens to you with a wisely watchful mind. Out of this will arise the power to be fully involved with events without feeling threatened by them.

When fearing anything we attribute to it a power which it does not possess in fact. So fear is a wrong move because it is untrue. You need not yield to anything untrue. Just release what is true in you.

The rescuing facts are as near as your own mind. Here is one of them. Cease to choose the way you now live and you cease to suffer from the results of that choice. Discuss with yourself this direct method of self-rescue.

EXERCISE IN HIGHER THINKING

People want to know what action to take in this or that situation. Esotericism provides the answer. Think of action as doing something totally different with your mind. Regardless of the situation, think of action like that. Do not act from impulsiveness or habit or from a desire to protect your present beliefs. Such actions drain away into nothingness, just as water is absorbed and wasted by the dry desert.

To think more clearly, to catch a fresh insight, to toss out a self-punishing belief — these are true actions. And they reflect themselves favourably in daily affairs.

For a healthy exercise in higher thinking, suspend judgment towards the ways you think. Do not conclude that your present mental movements are necessarily accurate or beneficial. Do not believe that your usual world of thoughts is the only world in existence. This leaves room for something higher than the habitual. That is what you really want — something higher than the habitual.

EXPERT TWISTERS

A village was inhabited by skilled craftsmen who twisted pieces of wire into figures of human beings and animals. Their appreciative customers referred to them as the Expert Twisters.

But the villagers were not happy. Commercial success had contributed nothing towards inner satisfaction. So they called in a teacher of esoteric truth, requesting, 'Please give us spiritual food.'

Knowing exactly what would happen, the teacher gave his first lecture. It happened. The Expert Twisters distorted everything they heard. Stated the teacher, 'The need to dominate others is unhealthy.' Someone in the audience called out, 'But the world needs strong leaders.' The teacher counselled, 'Stop living from a surface appearance of goodness.' Someone replied, 'I can't help it if my neighbour lives like that.'

The teacher pointed out, 'Your commercial habit of wire-twisting has crossed over into mind and heart. You expertly twist the truth into whatever you want it to be. See this in yourselves. Come to the next lecture with a sincere wish to no longer twist the truth. Let it be what it is – your deliverance.'

EXPLAIN HUMAN NATURE

'How can we find answers to the human dilemma in a minimum of time?'

'Explain human nature and you explain everything. For example, the less a man has changed himself the more his obsessive urge to change others. This explains the private despair of the public reformer.'

'You said it was necessary to go into action with our acquired knowledge. I am not sure what this means.'

'Action consists of permitting knowledge to erase a misconception. An example of this is to permit a crisis to reveal that we don't have the inner poise we imagined we had. This is healthy action. Knowledge without right action is like writing a letter but declining to walk out to post it.'

'Our study group is making a special study of esoteric laws. May I hear one of them to take back to the group?'

'An awakened man does not pursue sleeping men, for that is against esoteric law. The unawakened man must pursue the man who knows. His pursuit indicates an admission of need, and that admission is necessary.'

EXPLANATION OF HEARTACHE

Admitted Lloyd, 'I know there is something wrong when I make stern demands on others, but I don't understand it. I know very well it will cause a quarrel, but I still go ahead. Why?'

'Think it through. Anyone who believes that others should

conform to his personal wishes is saying that his mind alone has a right to exist. Even the simplest logic shows how egotistical and ridiculous this is. Be aware of how this self-centredness brings self-punishment. This is a first clue for living with your universal mind.'

The causes and cures of quarrels and heartaches in human relations are not mysteries.

We hurt each other because we are afraid.

We are afraid because we do not know who we are.

We do not know who we are because we have never investigated.

Investigate!

EXPLORATION OF HAPPINESS

A small boy was seated on the floor, reading a picture-book. From time to time he asked questions of his mother about the book. The mother finally realized that the boy could not clearly see the small details of the pictures. She told him to turn round and face the lamp, explaining, 'You are blocking your own light.' The next paragraph explains one way in which people block their own light.

A person obsessed with the need to be happy will never be so. The obsession is the obstruction. He does not really seek happiness, rather, he seeks for a condition which matches his personal idea regarding the nature of happiness. But happiness is not a mere idea, for one idea will always have competition from another idea. That is why the unhappy man chases for ever from one attraction to another. Happiness will come when he stops chasing, that is, when he stops thinking that an idea about happiness is the same as happiness. A man enjoying the sunshine does so without analysing it.

FACTS AND FANTASIES

The only true friends you have are the facts of life. Fantasies masquerade as friends, but desert you once they have heartlessly used you. Here are a few friendly facts:

Never listen to what your surface mind insists is good or bad, but listen only to what your deeper mind knows is good.

The only reason you need for seeking truth is because the truth is true.

Let something right happen inwardly, and you will have no concern over what happens outwardly.

If you want to see through other people, you must first see through yourself.

To change yourself, think of a disturbing circumstance or habit which you accept as necessary, then begin to question its necessity.

FALSE PERSONALITY

A teacher was about to deliver a public lecture. He instructed his disciples, 'Observe the audience carefully.'

During the question period of the lecture, one man challenged the teacher several times. The man obviously found considerable pleasure in making statements such as, 'I disagree with what you say,' and, 'I think I caught you in a contradiction.'

After the lecture the teacher explained to his students, 'This man is a familiar type of fearful person whom I recognized at once. Feeling threatened by the truth he tried to protect his ego by disagreeing. The man was saying that *his* ideas were superior, in fact, *he* should have been the lecturer. Do you know what was talking? His false personality, not his real nature. As long as he enjoys this false self he cannot help himself.'

FASCINATING LIGHT
Be aware of this: On the everyday level of people and events, there is no such thing as a missed opportunity. No matter what a man thinks about it, the winning of that desired money or that attractive person or that public honour can do absolutely nothing for his true life, so there is nothing to miss. We dimly suspect this, but must admit it into full awareness, which ends the agonizing pursuit. What an opportunity we have for becoming transformed men and women! Make up your mind to not miss this pearl of great price.

What you are doing all along is to pull aside decorated curtains which you did not see as curtains because of your hypnotic fascination with their fancy designs. But now you have caught a glimpse of light through a small crack in the curtains. This is your new and real fascination. Now, above all else, you want less curtains and more light.

FEARLESSNESS
'I don't want to be afraid any more. Who can teach me?'

'You can learn fearlessness only from a man who is not himself afraid.'

'Are there such men?'

'Though few, they exist.'

'How can I find a man immune to fear?'

'By having ten times the wish to be free of fear than you now have. Otherwise, you will be deceived by terrified men who pretend to be free.'

'Where can I start doing what is necessary?'

'Question every idea given you since birth.'

FEAR OF DISPLEASING PEOPLE
Many years ago an explorer in primitive Africa was leading an

expedition towards Victoria Falls. All along the way he was halted by petty tribal chiefs who demanded payment for crossing their territory. The explorer paid them with small items not necessary for the journey, but which the chiefs valued. So the caravan progressed.

Similarly, in inner exploration, payment guarantees progress. Payment consists of giving up anything misleading and useless.

When hearing about this principle, Lawrence gave it careful thought. Looking inwards, he tried to find something to give up. He found something — the fear of displeasing people. 'I never realized,' he commented, 'how anxious I was to gain and keep the approval of others. That is one slavery I will give up.'

Find your own ways to make payment, to give something up. Dare to give up self-concern. Be eager to abandon misleading thoughts. This will leave you in a different place than you were before.

FEELINGS OF FUTILITY

Have you ever wondered what to do when life seems pointless? Read the next paragraph with a mind that wants to know.

A feeling of futility is trying to tell you something of great importance. Listen to it. Do not be afraid to listen to its entire story, for only good can come from your attention. A feeling of futility serves the same purpose as feeling chilly on a cold day. Feeling chilly is not a scolding or a condemnation. It has no wish to make you miserable. It is simply nature's helpful way of saying that something must be changed. That is all. A feeling of emptiness and purposelessness can be wisely used to change the way we meet life, just as we change clothing to meet changing weather. So see moods of depression and aimlessness like this. That begins to change your psychological clothing, which keeps you comfortable in all kinds of conditions.

FEELINGS OF SHAME

Whoever has turned on his original light has transcended a sense of shame, regardless of wrong behaviour in the past. Shame is a part of egotism, for it maintains one's illusion of having an individualistic self apart from the Whole. Perhaps you know people who love to boast about past or present wickedness, while pretending to be sorry. The last thing the ego will do is to give up shame, for it uses shame to perpetuate its tyranny over the person. People would rather feel ashamed than feel nothing, for a lack of fiery emotions seems like a fearful void to those who misunderstand.

Now, to understand the nature of wrong behaviour is quite another response. To do this is to see it without the interference of the false self, therefore, egotism's grip is weakened. This is the beginning of good behaviour and of true conscience.

FIND YOURSELF

All the great religions and philosophies teach in their own words, 'To lose your life is to find it.' The meaning of this becomes increasingly clear to the student of esotericism. In summary, we must lose what we falsely believe is our life in favour of a wholeness which never needs to prove itself.

Asked Donald, 'How can I find myself?'

'Get yourself out of your own life, which means to detect and abandon the imaginary self-pictures by which most men live. Then you will be in your own life for the first time. Michelangelo practised a certain technique while painting. When working in dim light, he placed his candle inside a cup. This prevented his own shadow from interfering with his work. All of us somehow sense that all would be well if we could just get out of our own way. Think often about the meaning of this.'

FIRST SUCCESSES

Our early successes consist largely of faint hints of another world. An alert and receptive mind, determined to throw off the wrappings of life, senses this new universe. If reading,

'Man's problem is his meandering mind,' there is something within which feels the fact in that statement. Already the light has brightened. You then read, 'But any mind weary of wandering in the wilderness can return home.' That also produces a response, different and rightly encouraging.

At this very moment you are closer to these heavenly hints than you think. They are as close as your own eagerness to make contact. You are perfectly capable of contacting everything needed for spontaneous hours. Let yourself make contact. Do this by letting your mind run towards necessities, not towards demands.

Just catch your first glimpse. That is enough. Nothing will ever persuade you to go back to the old ways.

FIVE LESSONS

After observing his students for several days, a teacher gave five of them the lesson each needed the most.

'You must get over your terror of the truth. That is like a prisoner who fears the key to his cell.'

'I want you to see that you can please your true nature, or you can please your negative characteristics, but you can't please both.'

'You need more diligence, so take a lesson which does not make sense and study until it does.'

'I wish you to remember one fact for the rest of the day. You are the slave of those from whom you seek approval.'

'You must see that the battle is not against people and conditions, but against the wrong use of your own mind.'

FLOW OF LIFE

Suddenly ask a man, 'What do you value?' Watch his puzzled face. For a split second he will not know what to reply. Then, as memory and conditioning rush up, he will tell you. He may say, 'I value a worthwhile life,' or, 'I value exciting days.' He may not really mean what he says, for human beings tend to say whatever sounds the most impressive. But one thing is certain. The values arising from his acquired notions will be valueless — worthless to the man himself, though he may not see it.

Why? Because memorized values must always clash with the new and natural and changing flow of life. The man who values fame will be anxious if it fails to arrive or if it comes and departs. The woman who insists upon physical attractiveness will be sorrowful when it is not present.

Seeing through false values is both an interesting and profitable occupation for those who want to escape from them.

FOCUS ON REALITY
Suppose you are standing on a high hill with a friend. Below you is a small village with attractive homes and colourful fields. While looking through binoculars your friend says he can see his home quite clearly. You ask to have a look, so he hands over the binoculars with the instructions to aim towards the centre of town. Peering into the binoculars you see nothing but a blur. You realize what has happened. When taking the binoculars your fingers touched the focusing wheel, turning it away from the right position. When corrected, the binoculars reveal the home below.

We are out of focus with reality, which explains the blurs in our days. That is the explanation of human distress offered by every teacher of all ages and lands.

We possess the talent for correcting whatever prevents a clear view of ourselves and our actions. That is the encouraging solution offered by those who know.

FORGIVENESS
Confessed Gordon, 'I feel I may be unforgiven for past cruelties and neglects. Please help me.'

'Do not think about forgiveness from man-made ideas about it. They consist of assorted illusions, including self-serving sentimentality. Think from esoteric teachings. Start with the idea of self-forgiveness. This occurs each time conscious behaviour replaces mechanical and memorized behaviour. To say the same thing another way, forgiveness occurs by dropping the past to live only in the present moment. The eternal now has no past, therefore no guilt, therefore no need to even think about forgiveness.'

'What about forgiveness from those I have harmed?'

'Anyone you have offended who has found the light will understand all you have just heard, so he forgives you as he has forgiven himself. Those still in darkness, the majority of people, have no understanding of real forgiveness, so you can forget them. Truth has provided total forgiveness.'

FORTUNATE POSITION

When anguish becomes unbearable, you are in a fortunate position. Do not miss your good fortune. Do not try to escape the pain by emotional storms or by pleasant day-dreams or by any other distraction. Stick with the pain. Do not run away.

Do you see why? Follow closely. You cannot run away from suffering because there is no self which is apart from suffering. You are the anguish itself. You and anguish are the same thing. You cannot run away from pain because there is no division between you and pain. You see the impossibility of trying to run away from your own body, so you do not try. With equal clearness see the impossibility of running away from distress.

Once we see the impossibility of running away from anguish, a remarkable change takes place. So see just this much, after which a new self-clarity takes over to end distress.

FOUR ANSWERS

Mr and Mrs K. collected four written questions from the group, then read them aloud for the teacher to answer:

1. 'How can we know whether we are living from the truth instead of just talking about it?'

'You live the truth when you see no difference between having a truth-discussion with others and taking a pleasant stroll by yourself.'

2. Why do we pursue the bad, even while sensing its harm?'

'Because there remains parts of us which are still under the illusion that the bad is the good.'

3. 'Why does self-facing cause discomfort?'

'As a general statement we can say that it is the truth that hurts, but more exactly it is our resistance to the truth that hurts.'

4. 'What is an example of how we block our own liberty?'

'The faster a man nervously defends his wrong positions the slower will he find the hill which is above all nervously defended positions.'

FRESH HEALTH

Every person feels the truth of the counsel, 'The most sensible act you can perform in your life is to escape your own inner trap.' Many questions asked in classes indicate a growing awareness of this.

Walter said during an open discussion, 'You say that the understanding of emotional suffering ends it. What prevents understanding?'

'Suffering itself. Look deeply into the nature of suffering and you will see dozens of wrong moves. Suffering makes a person the centre of attention, including his own. It gives him a chance for public and private dramatics. He loves the false feeling of life supplied by anguish. Suffering is loaded with dangerous egotism, so neither glorify it or be sentimental towards it. As insight grows, a sufferer sees all this, and wants nothing more to do with it. Fresh health replaces suffering.'

FROM ANOTHER WORLD

An American farmer was walking through his fields one day when he sighted a rock lying beneath a cornstalk. The rock held his attention, for not only did it have an unusual appearance, but it seemed out of place in the cornfield. The farmer carried it home, studied it curiously, and finally set it in the front yard as a stepping-stone. One day the farmer had a visitor who was an amateur astronomer. The rock was equally attractive to the visitor, who examined it closely. It turned out to be a meteorite — a unique rock from another world.

We must recognize the existence within us of psychic powers from another world. Our recognition is our transformation.

FUNDAMENTAL MAN

We must see the difference between self-transformation and what is popularly called self-improvement. Everyone wants self-improvement, but only the daring and the wise seek self-transformation.

Self-improvement makes elementary changes. One can improve his memory or lose excess weight or learn a new skill for earning a living. Some of these are useful for daily affairs, but none can bestow self-command in a riotous world. In other words, the fundamental man does not change.

The fundamental man. Attention to that essential feature begins the process of self-transformation. So what must be done to activate this cosmic creativity? A man must study his daily ways to see just how he is acting against his own ease and naturalness, to see just where he has permitted confused thoughts to take the place of the clear thoughts possessed by his cosmic mind. This daily alertness changes the fundamental man, just as a motorist changes directions when noticing he is on the wrong road. When on the right road, we feel right.

FUNDAMENTAL RULE

Requested Harry, 'May we review an elementary question? How can a person change himself?'

'Remember the fundamental rule. No man ever changes his behaviour until clearly seeing self-defeating behaviour *as* self-defeating. He must observe how he really feels at the time he says or does something against his own nature. Equally important, he must not mistake the ego-thrill of wrong behaviour for happiness. It may take many shocks and frustrations, and a powerful pressure of pain before a man lets go of his pretence and his resistance to truth. He will let go fearfully at first – for he knows not what will become of what he calls his self – but he is breaking out of prison. No longer giving value to mere emotional excitement, he sees how he has been defeating himself. This is his first glimpse of a changed nature.'

GENUINE HELP

In human beings there is a gulf a mile wide between 'There is something wrong with me' and 'Well, I had better change myself.' The difference between the usual person and the extraordinary individual is that the latter sets about systematically and with endless energy to navigate the gulf. The others stand tearfully on the bank and complain that no one builds them a bridge.

The facts of life cannot be perceived by anyone who needs to have others on his side when seeing whatever he sees. Only by standing alone can he stand within the undivided universe which knows and explains the facts of life.

Anyone travelling the right road will have genuine help all along the way. His own secret forces will always be wherever he is, to guide and encourage. When confused by something he can assure himself, 'By working patiently with this to the very end, I will have psychic gold I never had before.'

GIGANTIC CONSPIRACY

Wayne told a group during an open discussion, 'A man has no idea of what he wants and then spends a lifetime trying to get it! That is my own biography up to now. What is wrong with us?'

Elaine responded, 'Mankind has entered into a gigantic conspiracy to keep everyone hypnotized. Look at the vacant faces you pass on the street and you will see how well the conspiracy has succeeded. We want to escape from it.'

Insisted a visitor, 'But surely things will improve with time and better organization. I don't understand your negative attitudes towards the human problem.'

Lew spoke up. 'It is not negative to face the fact that everything man has tried up to now has failed. It is negative to refuse to see the obvious. The quality of human life cannot be raised by the minds which have made it what it is. Destruction cannot be constructive. But human destruction always calls itself constructive, so the level remains the same. As Elaine said, we are here to end self-hypnosis.'

GLIMPSE OF REALITY
At the start we seek to set artificial personality aside long enough to let the real man appear, even for an instant. This glimpse reveals the difference between the troublesome artificial and the rescuing real.

A student in Oregon suffered from compulsive goodness. She described her condition as, 'For ever doing exactly what I did not want to do — with silent resentment.'

She was urged to thoroughly examine her motives for being so generous with her time and money. Doing so she reported, 'I behave generously because of a craving for applause from others. But this kind of generosity contains no real goodness because it secretly demands a reward. I sense where I am going wrong. I walk around with a mere self-picture of being a good person and so demand that others confirm it through appreciation of me. But being only an image, an illusion, it is ridiculous to try to confirm it. I need only abandon the image in favour of my real nature. I now glimpse the difference between artificial personality, with all its wars, and my really good true self.'

GOD
Said Audrey one evening, 'These classes are fascinating, but how does God enter into everything?'

'To answer that you must tell me what you mean by God. Everyone has a different idea as to the nature of God, but an idea about God cannot be God. This is why we have thousands of conflicting gods and religions on earth. These gods are merely projections of personal desires and fears. God has nothing to do with such division.'

Audrey nodded. 'Just that much is already helpful.'

'Clearness comes by realizing God as the Whole, the All. The mechanical part of the mind cannot know this Allness because it demands to be its own petty god — which fights cruelly with other petty gods. A Whole Mind knows God because it is One with itself.'

GOOD AND EVIL

Ruth wanted to know, 'Is man basically evil or is he good?'

'You will grasp this better with another approach. See man as *captured*. This is why esoteric illustrations tell about men who escape prison or who find the way out of a cave of robbers. But by what is man captured? Only by his own illusions of being in captivity. In reality, he is free now and for ever. But insight of this must come to him. So evil is the behaviour of an unconscious person, like a man having a nightmare who kicks out furiously. He is cruel because he is afraid. His injury of others is the painful explosion of self-injury. By seeing all this, he escapes his own captivity. Then, authentic goodness is his total nature.

GOOD CHEER

There is cause for good cheer. Through right action, the mind can set itself free. Right action consists of starting with part of the mind to enter the Whole Mind. A Whole Mind is freedom itself. Man's mistake is in believing that the part of the mind he now employs is the Whole Mind, which is like taking Denmark as the only nation on earth.

Taking the part as the whole. That is the rock in the road to be avoided. Memory is a good example of this mistake. Memory alone cannot bring freedom, also, misused memory leads us astray. We see this in people whose memories have been crammed with ideas about the nature of God, so all their lives they worship a cluster of memories they call God. God does not consist of memorized ideas. God is not the past and the part. God is the Present and the Whole.

So be of good cheer, for memory can start right action as soon as it receives self-explaining knowledge.

GOOD NEWS

Everything about the esoteric path is good news. Keep this thought in front of you at all times, but especially when feeling uncertain about a received idea or course of action. Many times in our early days we encounter ideas which seem foreign to us. In fact, the ideas are not at all foreign to our real nature, but because of our wanderings in strange lands, it appears that way.

So regardless of first impressions, good news is the only kind of news we ever receive. Suppose a man is told he must stop jumping into one excitement after another. He may assume that is bad news, for he uses emotional and social excitement as distractions from his anxiety. But it is wonderful news, for it is a first clue towards the healing of his anxiety. So whatever news comes your way, read it carefully until seeing the brightness which is always there.

GOOD START

You can start on the path exactly where you are right now. There is no other place to start anyway. Your present inner and outer circumstances, no matter how dark, are unimportant. At the start you are required only to start. The beginning might consist of an earnest questioning of your life as it now unfolds. It could be wonderment over an inspiring idea you read in a book. It might be a persistent urge to become another kind of person.

Progress can be compared with a path having a series of gates along the way. You go somewhere by passing through something. So whatever you meet is exactly what is good and necessary for your progress. So welcome every experience, regardless of how mystifying or annoying it may appear to be.

Simply start. Take any forward step. Now take the next step, whatever it may be. Proceed one step at a time every day. That is truly noble action.

GRAPE VINE

An orchardist noticed that a certain grape vine failed to produce much fruit. He had almost decided to waste no more water on it when the vine spoke up. 'Please,' it appealed. 'It is not my fault if I fail to supply an abundance of grapes. It is the fault of my surroundings. I will do just fine if you give me a shield from the hot sun.'

A shield was placed over the vine, but it did no better than before.

Over the weeks the grape vine pleaded for other changes in its environment. It requested the removal of some nearby rocks and asked to be surrounded by flowers. Its requests were granted but it failed to keep its promise to bear more grapes.

The orchardist finally woke up. He told the vine, 'It is not your surroundings which are wrong. It is your own nature. You are like some people I know. They never see that a change in environment is not a change in nature.'

GREATER POWER

An individual can go as far as he wishes. How can he generate greater power for advanced adventures? He can:

Want to tell the truth to himself.

See through myth parading as fact.

Not love to feel angry and indignant.

Be tired of playing games.

Guard against automatic assumptions.

Not accept the false comfort of conformity.

Know how little he knows.

Not live within a small corner of himself.

Question his cherished values.

Sense something wrong with noisy places.

Learn rightness by observing wrongness.

See how he stands in his own way.

Seek the meaning of psychic maturity.

Wish to be at home with himself.

GRIEF

'We are in a terrible predicament. At the same time as we cling to people we feel ourselves under their power to threaten our security.'

'You should be grateful to people who threaten what you call your security. They are teaching you an essential lesson. Be aware that any security which can be threatened is no security at all.'

'What about those who insist we should see only the good in people?'

'That is just another attempt to rearrange reality to fit one's flattering ideas of self-goodness. Good can come, but only by understanding the nature of the bad. Evasion prevents this insight.'

'You tell us to study how we attract our own grief. Some people find this hard to accept.'

'Look at Tom who gets hurt by Bill. You feel sorry for Tom, but do you ever ask why he associated with Bill in the first place?'

GROUP PROCEDURES

Members of a study group should take every opportunity for helping each other. The light one holds out for another is the same light guiding oneself.

One method is for a member to explain a particular idea to the others. He could start, 'I would like to explain to you the importance of sticking to the point — the point of self-awakening.' He then discusses the idea for a minute or two. He should speak simply, explaining the ideas as clearly as possible.

A second method is for the leader to request answers to his question. The leader might ask, 'Why is direct and personal contact with the truth essential?' Someone might reply, 'Because it is the only way to reach the harbour. The wise voyager takes directions from the sun itself, while the unwise man listens to what others tell him about the sun.'

Participants should feel no embarrassment at mistakes or hesitations when contributing their bit. Even a little extra light pushes back the surrounding darkness. That is what it is all about.

GROUP PROGRESS

Five members of a study group reported lessons they had learned over the months:

Lee: 'One of your freedoms is to have no need to explain yourself to others. This is the reward for having first explained yourself to yourself.'

Ellen: 'No man can demand the right to mess up his own life and then demand the opposite right that other people should repair the damage.'

James: 'Esoteric education is totally different from any other kind of schooling. For example, the moment I see I am wrong, I am right.'

Lucille: 'There is a great difference between hearing a truth and being healed by what we hear, depending upon whether we open an ear or open the spirit.'

Hugh: 'Persistence in search of the truth must be accompanied by a willingness to live what we have learned. A pianist is not judged by how long he plays but by how well he performs.'

GUIDEPOSTS

Let the guideposts of the following paragraph aid you and those with whom you share the journey.

A person seeking help usually makes dozens of blunders at the start. Having little discernment he rushes from one useless teaching to another. He is like an ill person who cannot see the emptiness of all the medicine bottles offered him. Nevertheless, he is taking right and necessary action, for he must actively seek a true source of help. Success depends upon his courage to refuse comfort or excitement in favour of trueness. He must not let his desire for security judge the accuracy of an offered teaching. He must increasingly permit his own intelligence to judge between accuracy and error. It is by this method that aimless thrashing finally moves in one creative direction.

GULLIBILITY

See the difference between knowledge and assumption. Because of emotional tension, this is not so easy to do at first. A woman who loses the man in her life may assume she knows the answer to her loneliness — another man. That is simply an assumption based on her anxious desire to escape loneliness. Since it is an assumption and not a known fact, she suffers from its false hope. Also, it may lead her straight into an unhappy relationship with another man.

Self-damaging assumptions can exist only when we fail to meet a challenging condition with a whole mind. An assumption fails to see the whole picture, for instance, it does not see the vast difference between a person's public appearance and his actual inner condition. So assumptions produce gullibility and regret. But a whole mind assumes nothing. Having no anxiety, it does not see the world through rose-coloured glasses. It sees things as they are, which is its ease and protection.

HAPPINESS

To sow the same seeds is to reap the same weeds. Even this simple law of nature is overlooked by those who ache over a habitually hopeless harvest. To gain something different we must do something different. How easy it is to criticize whatever goes contrary to our present beliefs rather than attempt to understand. How shallow it is to speak the word 'love' and not realize that the word is not the virtue.

Do what you should do instead of what you want to do. At first it arouses resistance, but the time will come when what you should do and want to do are the same thing. That stage is known as happiness.

Perhaps you would like to know how the truth makes you a different kind of person. With a mixture of wonder and appreciation you will see the difference in yourself for yourself. Here is one way in which you will be different: You will have the casualness of a person who has nothing to prove.

HEALING TRUTH

'How can I be different?'

'Be the way you are.'

'I don't understand.'

'You must always be the way you are because there is nothing else. Pretending to be different will chain but not change you. A sheep who imagines he is a lion is still a sheep.'

'But how do I change by being what I am?'

'By seeing what you are. See the difference between your real nature and your dozens of stage roles. When realizing the price you pay to be onstage, the roles fall away of themselves.'

'I see. Awareness of what I am changes what I am. But I fear such self-honesty will hurt.'

'The truth that hurts is the same truth that heals. Remember that.'

HEALTHY DESIRES

There are harmful desires and there are healthy desires. It is healthful to desire:

More light.
To live your own life.
Courage for self-facing.
Authentic assistance.
Freedom from raging thoughts.
Days without nightmares.
Casualness.
Non-interference from others.
To end self-doubt.
Silent power.
More natural strength.
Something truly different.

All these can be won. Nothing stands in the way of attainment except an insistence upon clinging to the old ways.

HEALTHY VIEWPOINT

'I want to change myself and my life!' Beneath their hourly activities, most people exclaim that. People are dissatisfied, doubtful, lonely. Unfortunately, most of them choose changes which change nothing. If you deeply wish to change your life, let the following thoughts serve as accurate guides:

Constantly examine the viewpoint from which you see life.

Society calls a man wealthy or successful or important. That is society's viewpoint.

Truth has no such viewpoint. It sees the man as he really

lives in his private mind. Truth sees him as a frightened human being whose fame and fortune do nothing to relieve his dreadful bewilderment and boredom. But Truth also sees him as someone capable of changing himself — if he adopts the Cosmic Viewpoint.

Never forget the existence of a viewpoint which sees things as they are. See life and see yourself from this healthy viewpoint.

HELPLESSNESS

Do you ever feel helpless? Have you ever tried living with feelings of helplessness just to see what happens? Try it. Simply live alertly with feelings of helplessness without doing a single thing about them. Do not try to be strong, do not resist or resent the condition. Do not seek relief from tension by asking advice from others — for they feel equally helpless.

Do this. A personal miracle will happen. By living fully with feelings of helplessness you destroy a trick that was being played on you. When you are totally helpless — and see this as a plain fact — the terror vanishes. Feeling helpless disappears because you now see that your real nature was never in danger and therefore needed no help at all. God does not need help. It was the imaginary self which felt threatened and which therefore cried for help. But seeing the non-existence of the false self ended the need for help. You do not need to save a non-existent person.

HIDDEN HOSTILITY

During a casual group discussion, Michael admitted, 'For many years you could not have talked to me about these ideas. The wall between my mind and reality was a yard thick. I had superbly deceived myself into believing that I already knew all the answers, and was therefore a normal and highly intelligent human being. I will tell you of one area where any attempt to help me would have aroused an emotional beehive. Had you ever told me I was hiding a lot of fierce hostility it would have made me hostile!'

The others smiled in understanding. Michael continued,

'Now I know why. My hostility was a fact, but a fact unacceptable to my precious and deceptive self-images of being a peaceful person. How clear it all becomes after a while. Anger is a sure sign we are hiding something. Also, I saw something else. Anger and fear go together. I was hostile because I feared the exposure of my pretences. This class helped me to see that exposure of pretence is not something to fear, but a sensible and effective medicine.'

HIGHER KNOWLEDGE

You are about to receive higher knowledge about human affairs. Review it often.

As strange as it sounds at first, an individual never causes anything to happen. Everything happens by the flow of cosmic action. While this cosmic action exists within each person, it does not belong to him personally, therefore, he is not the originator. Mr A does not really cause anything to happen to Mr B and Mr C. None of them possesses an independent 'I' capable of personal action. All action between them is simply universal cosmic action. Suppose the parts of an automobile were given human names, with a wheel called Tom and the battery called Sally. Wrong thinkers would credit the fictitious Tom and Sally with individual power. But Reality sees things as they are. It sees Total and Co-operative Action between the nameless parts. Were label-loving human beings to see things as clearly as Reality, human life would be different.

HIGHER LOGIC

Nothing good can be expected from a world which lives from external appearances. And that is the kind of world you inhabit.

You must seek a logic much higher than that employed by shallow society. For example, an economic solution is offered for an economic problem. Both the problem and the solution are a part of human illogic, so nothing good can result. It is like trying to cure a sick man by bringing another sick man into the room. Only higher logic can change anything.

Remember, this is personal and private work. So regardless of what other people do, always aim to think in a higher way than you find yourself thinking.

Why are we doing all this? Because this is the way to make life make sense. At last, life makes sense.

HIGHER PLACE

Misconceptions supply the illusion of travel, that is, they seem to take us somewhere. But we always find ourselves right back where we started, discouraged at the bursting of another beautiful dream. We feel lost, betrayed. But esoteric ideas are not like that. They always leave us in a higher place.

There is a sure method by which anyone can begin to solve the mysteries of life. He can see and bravely face whatever does *not* explain his personal dilemma. He might see at last that so-called experts and authorities conceal as many doubts as he does. Or he might realize that his usual mental movements always end up quarrelling with each other. He is now seeing the futile *as* futile. This lightens his load, providing a surer forward step.

It can be done. The land you have not entered as yet has been entered and conquered by others.

HOME AT LAST

Whoever has no idea as to how other people *should* treat him is someone who has found the Secret of Life.

Should includes demands destructive to both the demander and the object of his clamorous claims. The very demand is the damage to the demander. A man living from *should* still believes he possesses a personal and separate world which others should confirm and praise. The constant refusal of Reality to accept his illusion is his angry agony. When two such men meet a collision is inevitable. This happens millions of times a minute to the people on earth. Now you know why you read tragic headlines every day.

Freedom from *should* attracts unlimited psychic riches. One of them is the absence of tension. Tension exists when the imaginary self tries vainly to prove its existence by striving for something, whether wealth or sexual conquest or anything else. When true being replaces the imaginary self, striving ceases. We then feel we have arrived home at last, after a long journey.

HOMING INSTINCT

Said a seeker to a teacher, 'You say man is hypnotized, which accounts for all his ordeals. You also say that right self-work can awaken him out of his difficulties. Is there proof of this?'

'You are the proof.'

'In what way?'

'You have ordeals.'

'Yes, but that is only half of it. What about evidence for self-awakening?'

'You are the proof.'

'I fail to grasp your meaning.'

'You would not have come here unless a small part of you suspected the existence of another mental state. Call it a homing instinct, like that of a pigeon. This does not necessarily mean you want the answer. Multitudes of others have the same sensing, but do nothing about it. What will you do?'

HONEST CONFUSION

A famous man was once interviewed by a reporter. The man admitted, 'My thoughts are like odd characters in a fairy tale who have suddenly come to life in my mind. I have no idea of where they come from or of what to do with them. I confess to a confused mind.'

Any worthwhile teaching assists seekers to understand and abolish mental confusion. Seekers must do their part by honestly acknowledging their bewilderment. Admission of confusion is powerful medicine for it combats those unconscious attitudes which pretend to know the answers. Unconscious bluffing is an ally of confusion.

Honest confusion is like a disabled boat flying a distress flag. It attracts assistance. So think of a present confusion you may have. *That* can be ended. It makes no difference whether you believe it or not. What makes the difference in your favour is a willingness to let these teachings come to the rescue.

HOW COURAGE ARRIVES

Yes, it takes courage, but a sincere invitation to that virtue assures its delivery. Courage comes as needed, for every earnest request is supplied. You are then poised and confident, without even thinking about it, in places you never dreamed possible. But, of course, we are now attaining many heights we once thought impossible.

There is a particular place where courage races to the rescue. It is the stage in our journey where we refuse to choose our usual rewards, for they are now seen as attractive but empty packages. Now no longer choosing them, they no longer come. So we feel anxious at the absence of the familiar face, the thrilling activity, the pleasurable pursuit. With quivering apprehension we wonder whether the promised land has been just another illusion. We feel trapped, like a carpenter who is commanded to neither finish nor abandon a half-built house.

Wait. Courage will appear, and with it, a clear mind. You will see. You will see that uncertainty was a necessary tunnel to pass through, which produced a miracle. Out of your very honest uncertainty arose hearty courage and insight.

HOW HUMILIATION HEALS

Are you aware of your ability to make decisions in favour of yourself?

Decide to end inner conflict, then give no thought to the consequences of the decision. It is strange how a turn towards trueness arouses uncertainty. We insist upon fearing our own freedom! What we fear is the humiliation of all that has given us name and position, but it is the very crumbling of name and position that sets us free, for they were unconscious chains. Humiliation can be compared to an actor suddenly caught by the audience without his costume. It hurts for a moment, but then he remembers the man under the costume. By permitting total humiliation, we permit it to destroy the fantasy, leaving only the liberating fact.

HOW TO BREAK HABITS

People often ask questions about breaking unwanted habits, such as overeating and alcoholism.

All our usual thoughts about breaking a habit will only strengthen it. This includes so-called positive thoughts, such as plans for ending the habit. Mechanical thought cannot break a habit because thought itself is the habit. Thought cannot rise above its own level. A man in a pit cannot use himself to rescue himself. Something not of the pit is required.

What is this higher power? It is the silence residing between two thoughts. Watch your mind and you will glimpse this quiet interval between one thought and the next one. This silence is not mechanical thought, therefore it is not chained by habit.

Ponder everything you have read in this section. One morning the dawn will break, and you will see.

HOW TO PREVENT MISTAKES

There is a way to prevent the repetition of mistakes. Any time spent with this programme is worth more than gold.

Suppose you make a mistake on Monday. It will not repeat itself on Tuesday if you watch the mistake *as it happens*, wishing to be fully conscious of it. This means to understand everything involved in the error.

One man became involved time and again with the wrong people, including girl friends. All the relationships eventually ended with, quarrels and heartache. Wanting to break the painful pattern, he studied himself in action. He saw how he was driven by loneliness and insecurity to get mixed up with almost anyone. His full consciousness of cause and effect enabled him to drop the harmful habit. His new understanding showed him how to say 'no' to a worthless relationship.

Your new nature corrects mistakes. Let consciousness

release its power.

HUMAN TARGETS
Philip spoke up in the group. 'Sometimes I feel like a target struck by society's arrows. Piercing words and events strike throughout the day. I suspect self-centredness here. Your explanation would be appreciated.'

'There is just one way to get over feeling like a target. You must stop being an arrow. Target and arrow always go together, and both exist within you. When you insist upon shooting your arrow you also insist upon being a target. See this in small ways at first. If you shoot an arrow of hostility towards another person, you become the target for his returned hostility. Self-shocking honesty is required. A dishonest man always thinks he is the innocent target, never seeing how he makes targets of other people.'

HYPNOSIS AND REALITY
Asked Joyce, 'Please give us something we need.'

'When told you dwell in a state of psychic hypnosis, do not take it as mere words which seem somewhat critical. Take it as the actual condition which controls every minute of your day. You do not as yet know what it means to be hypnotized, for you dwell in imagination, not reality, but do not realize this. You do not know what it means to be hypnotized, for you have not as yet caught a glimpse of the awakened state. Try to snap yourself out of the spell, after which comparison will clearly reveal the fact of psychic hypnosis.'

'How can we see and snap this unconscious spell?'

'By regularly standing outside of yourself and looking back at your daily behaviour. With tremendous honesty, see your need to feel superior to others, see how you fear disturbance of your favourite ways, see how little you really know about yourself. Each sincere effort at this changes the kind of human being you are.'

IDENTIFICATION

Begin today to comprehend the enormously important idea called *identification*. Your understanding will sweep away a thousand difficulties in a flash.

To identify means to believe that something gives you an identity of some kind. You can identify with anything — money, sex, public prominence, your own thoughts. A man exclaims, 'See! I achieved my goal, therefore, I have an identity as a successful man.' In a gigantic blunder, he mistakes a mere idea about himself as being himself. And that blunder causes dozens of other errors, including fear of failure.

A very common form of identification is to identify with external activities. By chasing round and getting involved, a man tries to convince himself of the importance and usefulness of what he is doing. He deceives himself with the self-description, 'I am a dynamic and impressive man.' But his nightmares know better.

Esoteric wisdom urges him to slow down and take a look at the tragic trick he is playing on himself. That alone will save him from himself.

IMITATION

Imitation is always unconscious. A person imitating another's ideas or behaviour patterns is unaware of doing so. He insists his ways are both original and independent. He will resist being told otherwise, for his cluster of imitations have hardened into what he calls his 'I' and 'me'. The last thing he will permit is the destruction of what he calls his 'individuality'. Among other errors, he fails to realize that by borrowing another man's habits he also borrows that man's problems.

When you are with people, watch how imitation operates. Someone uses a fancy phrase, such as, 'Man's inhumanity to man.' A hearer is so impressed he can hardly wait to repeat it in order to make a good impression for himself.

Realization of an imitation life must precede the arrival of real life.

IMMUNITY TO INJURY

At a Saturday class, Helen said, 'Last week you urged us to build more self-honesty. I have been trying to succeed. Now I am sure there are many blunt truths about ourselves we need to face. May we hear one of them?'

'Whatever is wrong with other people can do you no harm unless the same thing is wrong with you. Do you see how a certain cosmic law operates here? You can get hurt only as long as you occupy the same psychological level as the person who hurts you. Rise above that level and you are immune to injury. An aeroplane passenger cannot be hurt by rocks tossed on the ground.'

'I am sure that all of us here grasp that with our intellects,' said Helen. 'Now we have to feel it with our whole being.'

'Do you now see why you are given all these blunt facts?'

'Why?'

'So you won't walk out of here into trouble.'

IMPOSSIBILITIES

One way of describing man's blunder is to say he attempts to do the impossible. He tries to make illusions look like realities.

He wants the excitement of worldly success without the fear of wordly failure. This is impossible, for life gives and takes naturally. He can rise above these opposites to true success.

He loudly declares his wish to get along with others, never seeing that this is impossible until he gets along with himself. He is deluded by thinking there can be a difference between his inner and outer worlds. There is only one world.

He tries to twist truth to fit self-interests. Impossible. Truth will not bend. Instead of trying to change truth, he must let truth change him.

Through true magic, the sighting of the impossible also reveals the possible — self-rescue.

INFORMATION AND INSPIRATION

The teachings in this book fall mainly on the mind and upon the emotions. For learning to take place, both must be open to the lessons. It is as important to understand with the feelings as well as with the intellect. Both must develop together and equally in order to maintain balance. A person dominated by his intellect is a repetitious tape-recorder. An individual commanded by his emotions is an unpredictably erupting volcano.

Happily, the growing stability of one part reaches over to steady the other part. It is like two horses who co-operate perfectly in pulling forward together.

The mind receives practical information. The feelings receive empowering inspiration. The section you are now reading is informational, while a later section, *Invitation to Refreshment*, is inspirational. See the difference in the two, then welcome both information and inspiration.

INNER AND OUTER

'There is a teaching I wish to grasp more fully,' stated Alan. 'The inner and the outer are the same. What does that mean?'

'Start by examining your relationship with yourself. What is it like? Do you have inner quarrels? Are you torn back and forth? This is your self-relationship. Now look outward. You will see that your relations with people and events are exactly the same. They must be. A wolf is a wolf, indoors or out. Dressing him in a wool coat does not make him a lamb. Now see the cheery side. As you change inwardly through self-insight, you change outwardly also. You have no quarrel with anything, for you have no quarrel with yourself. Is that worth finding?'

INNER WORK
In a temple in Tibet, a teacher was urging his students to be more receptive to truthful principles. As a visual lesson the teacher took a drinking glass and stuffed it with paper. Holding out the glass he instructed a student, 'Fill this with water.'

'Because of the condition of the glass,' replied the student, 'it cannot be done.'

Shaking the paper from the glass, the teacher asked, 'Can it now be done?'

The students understood the lesson.

Careless association with society as it now operates is enough to guarantee a stuffed mind — stuffed with the pompous and the frenzied and the stupefying. Where is room for the unaffected and the poised and the comprehensible?

Our inner work is a ridding process.

INNOCENCE
When anyone condemns you, silently ask him, 'Who gave you the authority to judge me? By judging me you claim to be superior to me. Where did you get this sense of superiority? Honestly, now, what are you really like inwardly? Have you ever judged yourself?' Say this without anger. Say it with a calm mind which wants to see things as they are.

This is a good start, but you must go on from there. What you have done up to this point is to free yourself of the illusion that one unawakened human being is better than another. Keep in mind that all sleeping human beings are equally unjust. Do not be deceived by external appearances by which individuals and groups claim rightness for themselves while attributing evil to others.

Having freed yourself of condemners and condemnations, go on from there. Study your actions to see just where you may be walking in your sleep instead of performing conscious actions. Then, finally, you will see that innocence alone knows what life is all about.

INSTANT HEALING
'We need to know more about raging emotions.'

'They are heat without light. You need not fall under them. Do not unknowingly consent to going under. That is half the victory.'

'You once said we can call the bluff on anxious feelings. What did you mean?'

'If you will look long enough at what frightens you it will get frightened and run away.'

'How can we test the ideas by which we live?'

'Does your philosophy change you? If not, change your philosophy.'

'I don't know the meaning of authentic strength.'

'You are truly strong any time you are not negative.'

'How long will it take to solve ourselves?'

'Esoterically, time has no power for self-healing. Healing is instantaneous. The moment of understanding is the precise moment of healing.'

INTELLIGENT PROCEDURE
A new class was formed in Minnesota. On the first night the teacher stated, 'This is the place to ask questions you would not ask any other place.'

Accepting the invitation, Harvey said, 'The question haunting me can be asked in just four words. Why am I afraid?'

'Why are you afraid? Because beneath exterior appearances of strength and confidence you are aware of the thin thread holding you to what you call your security. You know very well how a sudden change in circumstances could drop your surface happiness into the basement. Why don't you simply examine fear instead of fearing it? Has that highly intelligent procedure ever occurred to you? Many people never consider that simple solution. Why do you assume you must fear fear? Why not let insight set you free? That is why we have started these classes.'

INTELLIGENT SELF-ACTION

As an experiment in self-awakening, let other people behave towards you in any way they wish. Make no attempt to change or influence their behaviour. Neither resent what they do nor talk about them to others.

What is this all about? It is all about liberation. You are as free from other people and their behaviour as you are free from yourself. It is not their actions which really bother us; our trouble is our own insecurity which demands that they keep us safe and happy by doing what we want. So it is the individual who must change, not his relatives and friends.

As you let others behave as they want — which they will do anyway — an interesting change occurs within. In astonishment, you realize that *your demand on their behaviour is the only cause of your own anxiety*. They had nothing, really, to do with your distress.

This is what is known as intelligent self-action.

INTELLIGENT VOYAGING

In the days of sailing ships a schooner was caught in a mild storm off the coast of Scotland. One of the passengers was a young school teacher on her way to a new assignment in a coastal village. Worriedly, she asked the captain, 'Is it possible we might miss the harbour?'

The captain assured her with a smile, 'We may stray a bit, but the harbour can never be lost.'

Safety is always possible because your real nature can never lose itself. So have no concern if you cannot at present apply all these projects to your individual conditions. Just be diligent in learning your lessons in psychic navigation. You may forget your destination many times during the voyage, but your authentic nature will not forget. Ally yourself with what is right in you at every appearance of rightness, such as the urge to discover facts for yourself. That is intelligent voyaging.

INTENSE INTEREST

During a group meeting in New York, everyone was asked to

make comments which would brighten the light.

Bruce was the first to speak up. 'When first attending these meetings I was shy and nervous. Not sure what I was getting into, I sat here with an apprehensive mind. But my timidity was quickly replaced by an intense interest in what we discussed. Someone — I think it was Susan — made an excellent remark. She said that man yearns to harmonize with his real nature, just as a poet seeks a second word to rhyme with the first. That struck home. That was what I had been trying to do for years. I sensed there was authentic help in this group.'

Bruce shook his head and laughed lightly. 'The new student wonders how he can ever give up the attractive dangers in his life. The advanced student wonders how he ever kept his sanity while embracing them!'

INTERESTING ADVENTURE

Visualize yourself with a large map of a country you intend to visit, perhaps Australia. It is a very detailed map, filled with interesting and helpful information. Wishing to learn all about Australia, you settle down to study the map, but meet a problem. When the map was given to you it was tightly folded, and in some way the sections are stuck together. You succeed in loosening one of the folds, which provides your first peek at the country. With patient work you unfold another section which supplies more information. Each unfolding adds more awareness of the nature of Australia. Finally, the entire map is spread out before you. Now you know everything you need to know.

Our interesting adventure is to unfold ourselves to a full and valuable view of our total nature.

INTERNAL UNITY

A small boy suddenly found himself interested in the birds that visited his yard. He asked his mother endless questions about their nature and their habits. One morning, as the boy watched, the mother set out several bits of food for the birds. Looking at the biscuit crumbs, nuts, and other foods, the boy asked, 'How do you know which of those foods the birds like?'

'I don't know,' replied his mother, 'but the birds know.'

Every person has a natural intelligence which knows what is good for the person and what is not, but it must be awakened and activated.

When we act with just one part of ourselves we sense the strain and the incompleteness of that action. This happens when the face cheerfully greets others at the office, while the heart is secretly heavy. There is another way! As our fragmented parts come together to form internal unity, everything we do is done with everything we have. Then face and heart, word and feeling, action and reaction, work as one, and our cheerfulness is complete.

INTERRUPTIONS

Dennis commented, 'You say that expansion comes by interrupting our habitual ways. I sense the rightness in this, but what about the displeasure we feel when comfortable routines are interrupted?'

'Suppose you are sitting quietly, listening to dreamy music. A friend suddenly enters and shuts off the music, cutting off your pleasure. You may be disturbed at first, but then he tells you something. You hear that you must get going in order to make your aeroplane flight. Seeing the higher necessity, you lose interest in lower pleasure. That is how you should see the interruptions of daily routines. See them as friendly messages about a higher life, for that is what they are.'

'That is a unique way of looking at it.'

'That is why it works.'

INTUITION

Much of what is said about intuition is nonsensical and misleading. It usually appeals to what people want to believe about themselves. Tell someone he possesses rare powers of intuition and his wish to believe it robs him of all sensible examination of the subject. Such so-called powers are a combination of self-dramatizing self-deception, emotion-alized imagination and lucky guesses. The tragedy is the person's inability to see that his assumed powers have no practical value whatever. He still goes through his day in dazed worry.

True intuition is the natural outcome of consistent self-work which gives no place to delusions. Characteristic of highly developed men such as Christ, Buddha, Lao-tse, it is accompanied by goodness, decency, conscience. Such men were able to see things as they are, instantly, without conditioned thought.

True intuition first appears to sincere seekers as a brief glimpse of another way, as a faint hint of a new world. There is no mistaking its realness and freshness.

INVITATION TO REFRESHMENT

A thirsty wanderer in the desert was in despair over finding water. He struggled frantically from one hilltop to the next in an effort to sight a stream which was supposed to be in the region. His eyes searched in every direction, but without success.

While staggering through some dry bushes, his foot caught on a branch, spilling him to the ground. Exhausted and dejected, he remained there, listening to the surrounding silence. Suddenly, his head jerked upwards. He heard something new. It was the faint but definite sound of running water. Strengthened by the sound, he followed it all the way to a clear and cool stream of water.

Our very exhaustion can place us in a position to find what we really want and need. A silent but alert mind can hear the first faint invitation to abundant supply and refreshment.

J

JASMINE

A woman of ancient Asia was planning to emigrate with her family to a new land. Finding pleasure in gardening, she wished to grow a fragrant flower in the new country where they would settle. Visiting the village market, she asked the merchant for a flower having a rich fragrance. Holding up several plants, the merchant asked her to inhale their fragrance. Pleased by their scents, the woman purchased several plants and took them home.

But when the plants lost their fragrance during the next few days, the woman returned with them to the merchant. Hearing her story, he laughed and explained, 'Ah! I see! I thought you wanted a short-term fragrance. The plants I sold you were dipped into an inexpensive perfume. Their scent is artificial. That is what most people want. After brief pleasure they throw them out.' Holding up a plant with attractive white flowers, the merchant exclaimed, 'This is what you want. Jasmine! The jasmine plant has its own perfume. Take it anywhere. It will retain its richness.'

Be your own richness. It will endure.

JEWEL OF JAPAN

An inventory was once made of the imperial Japanese jewels. The royal treasure had been kept in a guarded building called the Shosoin. For nine hundred years the jewels had rested in the Shosoin, never seen by the public. When a string of amber beads was examined, one bead in the centre of the string appeared to be different from the others. The accumulated dust of centuries was washed off the beads, and the centre stone was examined with deep curiosity.

The examiners found a treasure within a treasure. The special bead was not made of common amber, as were the other beads. It was a high-quality pearl of pink-green colour. For hundreds of years the unique pearl had been mistaken for a piece of amber — but no longer.

No matter how long we have lived in a mistaken identity, self-examination can reveal our true and tranquil nature.

JIGSAW PUZZLE

Suppose a child is given a jigsaw puzzle and told, 'Set the pieces together rightly and you will have an attractive picture.' The interested child works on the puzzle but cannot get the pieces to fit. But trusting the person who gave him the puzzle he struggles to create the picture. But frustration builds pressure.

Suspend the child's story for a moment to see the similarity between his problem and man's baffling condition. Human beings have a life-problem. Authorities have assured them of success in working it out. But nothing works. Frustration builds tension and hostility.

Persisting carefully with the puzzle, the child makes an astounding discovery. The pieces belong to two entirely different puzzles! The difficulty itself was false. The authority he trusted was both wrong and careless.

That is what man must see. The problem itself is false. There is no need for fame and fortune. There is only a need to be a real person. We are not required to be young or attractive or desirable. We are invited to flow in casual harmony with our own true nature.

JOIN YOURSELF

If you have ever tried to listen to two people who were both talking to you at the same time you will have a good idea of man's divided nature. He is torn between dozens of society's noisy and contradictory voices, each claiming to be right and helpful. By listening to them he denies himself the right to hear his own intelligence which is always ready with true counsel. So ignore the voices. Listen only to the inner voice. Practise self-listening. What is the inner voice trying to tell you?

When scientists all over the world hear of a dangerous sickness threatening mankind, they join forces to combat it. That is the action of the alert individual. Instead of presenting a weak and divided nature to the world, he stands firmly by joining his own psychic forces.

For a topic of discussion in a study group, ask the question, 'What does it mean to join yourself?'

JOLT YOURSELF INTO NEWNESS

Battle energetically against usual habits, which means to understand them. There are certain parts of the mind which like nothing better than to sit back and take the course of least resistance. You must jolt them out of complacency, make them join you in the battle for self-conquest. Perhaps you see a reluctance in yourself to drop useless thoughts, such as running a past event through your memory, over and over. While gaining a peculiar pleasure from this mental movie, you also realize how it drains your mind. Go against it with conscious effort. Deliberately interrupt the mechanical movie. Jolt yourself. Declare, 'The reason I want to do this is because certain parts of me do not want to do it.'

See the new rightness in this practice. See how it is really different from usual ways, so it is certain to produce an unusual life. Join others who have had the courage to jolt themselves into newness.

JOURNAL OF A WINNER

One man who won his higher goals allowed few people to see parts of his secret journal, which read:

'Darkness cannot stop a refreshing breeze, nor can negative society block a sincere spirit.'

'While people still misunderstand, they cannot give up a wrong action, but with insight, a wrong action gives them up.'

'A great book or lecture is great only to those with budding cosmic greatness.'

'No man remains apart from life-liberation without the consent of one part of his mind, which is why self-study is essential.'

'There is complete agreement between cosmic principles and the accurate findings of science.'

'Like city lights, human beings are connected with a central and single source of power.'

'Never disconnect *action* from *awareness* and your ways will be right.'

JOURNEY TOWARDS SUCCESS

Requested Harold, 'Please give us a technique for more spiritual success.'

'Sacrifice false pleasure. Do this by first becoming aware of the damage of living in false pleasure. Suppose you have some information wanted and needed by another person. Withholding it from him may give you feelings of power and superiority. That is self-damaging false pleasure. Sacrifice the feeling by giving him the information. That removes a barrier on the journey towards success.'

Lillian raised her hand. 'What is true pleasure?'

'True pleasure consists of doing whatever your real and whole nature wants to do. Having none of the vanity and strain of artificial pleasure, it rolls merrily along, casually, carefree. Drop false pleasure and the authentic will reveal itself. It wants to be known by you.'

JOURNEY WITH LIGHT

An anxious man was stumbling and falling down a dark road when he met a stranger. The bruised man asked the stranger, 'Can you show me how to travel this road without so many hurts?'

The stranger nodded towards an object the man held in his hand. 'What is that?' the stranger asked.

'I don't know,' confessed the distressed traveller. 'Though I have no idea of its purpose I feel an urge to keep it.'

'That,' informed the stranger, 'is a lantern. It will show you how to travel safely.'

'But a lantern has light. This object is dark.'

'Only because you have not made an effort to uncover it. The light is there all right, but you must personally liberate it.'

'How can I do that?'

'By no longer loving the dark way. Oh, yes, you are quite fond of your bruises. The evidence is obvious. You prefer to endure your hurts instead of questioning their necessity. Cease to cherish your present ways. Each time you do this you liberate more light.'

JOY IN DISCOVERY

As part of your programme for progress, be aware of how words can be used to distort the facts. Men and women who fail to understand their minds use words as buckets of paint of different colours. White is painted over to appear blue; orange is covered by a coat of green.

Words are commonly misused when describing human characteristics. They are especially misleading and hazardous when used to flatter the weak and the foolish. A man with a neurotic need to dominate and hurt others is credited with being a firm and just authority. A woman afraid to be alone with herself is referred to as an outgoing personality who loves to be with her many friends. An obsession with self-centred fantasies is called a strong personal faith. Persistent greed for self-glory is called admirable courage in the face of obstacles.

A mind that takes a joy in new discoveries inquires constantly, 'Am I letting words distort the facts? If so, it will stop.'

JUDGE OF AUTHENTICITY

There was once a wise man known simply as the Judge of Authenticity. He counselled seekers who wished to know whether their new teachers could really help them unravel the mysteries of life. One morning he spoke in turn to four visitors.

'You approached that teacher because he was recommended by friends. Does he have something within himself worth recommending?'

'You heard someone who was surrounded by mindless multitudes. Cease to believe that crowds indicate authenticity.'

'You were attracted to that teacher by your own reckless desperation for answers. The unwary are easily exploited.'

'You have found a dynamic human personality who impresses you. Do you want to be impressed or rescued?'

A seeker asked, 'But how can we be sure of a teacher?'

'Dare to teach yourself the first few lessons, such as the need for self-dependence and the value of simplicity. This will develop your capacity to recognize a true teacher when he comes along.'

JUDGMENT AND AWARENESS

Man thinks he possesses clear and accurate judgment. It is one of his most disastrous illusions. Man is both the cause and the victim of this illusion.

Bring up any subject — religion, politics, social schemes — and a man leaps to his feet with loud opinions. The fact is, he knows nothing, absolutely nothing. He is a talking parrot who has not the slightest awareness of being one. Anyone trying to tell him about his stupendous ignorance is scorned or ignored.

True judgment consists of seeing things as they are, not as the individual has been taught to see them. An absence of conditioned self-interest is essential to the reign of true judgment. Craving and deceit and possessiveness distort clear judgment which can exist only in a pure atmosphere.

Only awareness of lack of judgment can begin to awaken cosmic judgment. And only self-honesty can awaken awareness.

JUNGLE OF PRETENCE

Pretence must be clearly seen as a disadvantage. One harmful pretence is to act as though one does not care about something which is really quite irritating. This is repression and division, causing tension. There is a carefree land, but it exists on the other side of the jungle of pretence, which must be explored.

Let your mind guard against an attempted invasion by all kinds of unworthy thoughts. Never doubt its power to repel harmful ideas. Because of daily defeats we assume that the mind is inferior to whatever happens to us. This is a wrong assumption. We simply lack knowledge of the mind's actual supremacy. The needed knowledge can be won. So let your mind admit only the high and the noble, just as a sea-wall permits only the higher waves to splash over to the other side.

KEEP YOUR DAY SIMPLE

A complex mind cannot understand simple ideas. Only mental simplicity has contact with simple ideas, in fact, the two are really one. Simplicity *is* understanding.

The simplification of your own life frees you from the complexities which chain other people around you. You can be in daily association with confused people, understanding them perfectly, and being personally unaffected by the problems they have not as yet solved for themselves. This peaceful position is a natural outcome of self-simplification.

Take a commonly bothersome belief and work on it. Take the idea that the thoughts of other people can harm you. That is absolutely false, so determine to see it as false. When a person gets hurt it is not the thoughts of others which do it, but the person's own wrong thoughts about their thoughts. Self-correction is total correction. Others may have harmful thoughts, but mental maturity provides immunity from them. A fox may be dangerous, but not to a lion.

KEY TO SELF-CONQUEST

When three students returned from a study session their teacher questioned them in turn:

'What did you read?'
'A book of religion.'
'What did you read?'
'A volume on philosophy.'
'What did you read?'
'Myself.'

'Ah!' the teacher exclaimed. 'You are getting it!'

You can lead an elephant in front of a man and if he does not want to see it he will not see it. He will see the elephant only if it gives him pleasure or helps to avoid pain. A true man makes it a point to see what his negative parts do not want to see, which eventually banishes the negative parts. Learn to read yourself. That is the key to self-conquest.

KIDNAPPED MANKIND

Imagine two men kidnapped by bandits and taken to a desert where they are forced to work for their captors. After several weeks they become somewhat accustomed to their captivity. But one of them finally sees an opportunity to escape. When informing his friend of it he hears the astounding reply, 'Leave here? Not me. I am staying.'

'Staying!' gasps the other man. 'But *why*?'

'It is a matter of loyalty and gratitude,' comes the explanation. 'After all, these men have fed and clothed me over the weeks. Also, they have relieved me of the responsibility of thinking for myself. You know, loyalty and gratitude are great virtues.'

An incredible scene that could not happen? It happens in the psychological world all day long. Accustomed to their chains, people feel false loyalty and gratitude towards their captors. The good news of liberation makes little if any impression on their minds. They cannot see their slavery for they call it security. Only those who call slavery slavery can escape.

KINDNESS

During a class discussion on human ways, a businessman asked several questions. One of them was short and to the point: 'Why do people cause so much trouble to people?'

He heard, 'Stop and think about it for a minute. What kind of man does not cause problems to others? Obviously, it is a man who is not a problem to himself. He has no inner pressures to overflow and hurt others. What conclusion do you reach from this?'

The businessman answered, 'The only way to be truly considerate of others is to straighten ourselves out.'

Few people really grasp the lesson you have just read. They do not see that authentic self-kindness and authentic other-kindness are the same thing, for both flow from the same inner nature. Where does real kindness begin? It begins with individual permission for the truth to enter and heal the inner condition.

KING AND SUBJECTS

There was once an insignificant man with a greedy obsession to become king of the land. Through trickery and violence he fought his way to the throne. One day a stream of visitors came before him.

The first was an army commander who requested a promotion and special favours. To ensure the commander's continued loyalty, the king agreed to the promotion.

Next came a powerful businessman who put pressure on the king to grant him a valuable piece of public land. Though fearful of public protest, the king agreed, for he profited personally from the country's business.

Then came the king's unpleasant wife who angrily demanded to be taken along on the king's future travels. Knowing she knew his many dark secrets, the king resentfully consented.

That evening the exhausted king flung himself into a chair to groan, 'Ah! I am the slave of my subjects.' He added philosophically, 'However, it does prove one thing. A good man is often the victim of greedy people.'

KINGDOM WITHIN

People do not find it easy at the start to accept the great fact of the kingdom of heaven within. Born and raised in a psychological wilderness, men and women know only the nature of the wilderness. Anything above that is the strange and the unknown. Tell them of another region and they either reject it outright or distort it to suit their fancies and preferences. Many people agree intellectually, taking the inner kingdom as an interesting and stimulating religious theory. But it is not a theory. It is a spiritual certainty, but one requiring individual discovery.

Sense the kingdom within. That is the same as coming home to yourself. It is the same as remembering your original nature. This remembrance comes dimly at first, expanding swiftly or slowly according to individual receptivity. It is like a man visiting the countryside scenes of his boyhood. He tries to remember the location of a favourite tree he used to climb, which remembrance comes as he strolls and thinks.

KINGLY CONDITION

Think deeply about the following guides until they lead you all the way to a kingly condition.

When confused about the best course for your life, do not battle that confusion. Make no attempt to clear your mind by making impulsive choices or by seeking allies for the battle. That is like fighting fog with your fists. Nothing good can happen.

When puzzled, do not do what you usually do. This is of utmost importance. Bewildered people cry out in desperation for an answer, which is then supplied by their own habit-thinking — which is always wrong. They might attract something which appears to relieve the crisis, but they are now simply confused in a new way. Sooner or later the sufferer is right back where he started, only sadder, for another pretty bubble has burst.

When remaining quiet, still, not battling, the disorder disappears. Why? Because confusion comes from habitual and mechanical thinking. When mechanical thought stops it can no longer create confusion. In that quiet space is clarity.

KNIGHT IN SHINING ARMOUR

As part of a class discussion, Ronald was asked to speak about himself. He began, 'I know how hard people fight the rescuing facts. I know because I battled them myself for many miserable years. Mythology tells of some men who turned to stone just by gazing at the frightful face of Medusa.

Just so do men become hardened against truth by staring at fame and fortune. A short time after timidly entering these studies, I saw clearly why people are so touchy, so sensitive. I realized why the smallest criticism is taken as a terrible insult to their good names. The reason is this. Jump on a toy balloon and you will hear a bang. Most people are empty balloons. Strangely, they defend their very emptiness. The greater the vacuum the louder the explosion of indignation. 'You are looking,' Ronald laughed, 'at a punctured balloon.'

Ronald concluded, 'As a boy I yearned to be a knight in shining armour seeking adventure. I never dreamed the quest would be an inward one.'

KNOCK LOUDLY
When knocking on the door to self-knowledge, knock loudly. Have no timidity. You will be neither criticized nor refused when boldly seeking admittance. Truth loves the sincerely persistent person who will not stop knocking until the door opens. Let the knowledge in the next paragraph circulate throughout your mind. That will be a loud knock.

One way to explain human carelessness is to say that a man lets someone else represent him. This he does quite unconsciously through submissive involvement with individuals and organizations. He never represents himself, his real and independent nature, though he is convinced he does. He can continue to let others speak for him, or he can learn to speak for and from himself, but he cannot stand on both sides at once. This is known quite well by the man who really represents himself.

KNOW FROM YOURSELF
A teacher of esotericism practised a certain technique for raising the consciousness of his students. From time to time, while listening to the remarks of someone in class, the teacher asked the student to pause for a moment. 'You have just made a good statement,' said the teacher, 'but I wish to know something. Did you say it from yourself or from someone else? Here is what I mean. Suppose that idea had

never before been spoken or understood by anyone on earth. Could you still have said it?'

This challenge helped a student. It enabled him to distinguish between quoting from memory and knowing from his original nature.

Know from yourself! That is the great state.

Reflect upon the following thoughts. Only when a man knows from his whole and united self can he *do* what he knows. For example, anyone can talk about love, but to truly express love a man must reside above the level of mere words. He must reside on the level of cosmic wholeness.

KNOWLEDGE FOR POWER

A manufacturer had a pattern by which he created a special kind of towel for the beach. The pattern produced defective towels. The manufacturer broke the pattern. No more defective towels appeared.

You must break the pattern. You must smash the pattern of your present life. There is no use trying to repair the pattern. It cannot be repaired, for defects are everywhere. It must be broken and tossed out once and for all.

A challenge? Of course. Everything within you will rise up in fearful protest. Opposing thoughts will try to deceive you in a thousand ways. They will slyly whisper that you are already on the right road, so there is no need to change anything. Or they will declare that it is a hopeless situation, insisting that sorrow and despair are man's inescapable prison.

But now you know. You know what to expect. This knowledge is power to ignore these dishonesties and pass onwards.

KNOW YOURSELF

When knowing yourself it is really quite easy to take care of yourself. Burdens arise when we insist upon taking care of property not belonging to our natural self. We take on unnecessary tasks because of failure to see them as such.

Take someone with a need to feel valuable to others. This

will also include the need for appreciation and compliments. So to win these feelings he sacrifices himself to others. He submits to the wishes or demands of others as a trade, a bargain. He agrees, 'I will do what you wish if you will occasionally make me feel liked and loved.'

Having traded his psychic integrity for a few sparkling beads of approval, he must now carry the self-imposed burden. Its wrongness is sensed, but he does not understand how it started or how it can be ended. He lacks self-knowledge.

When knowing yourself it is really quite easy to take care of yourself.

LAND OF LIGHTNING

Imagine a house in a stormy region. It is struck by lightning and damaged. The house shares the responsibility for being struck. Its very existence in a stormy land contributed to the disaster. The lightning was attracted to the house because the house was there.

It is possible for the house to avoid the punishing bolts of lightning. It can be moved to another location, to a land where lightning is not a surrounding threat.

So here is the answer to man's wailing outburst, 'Why does life give me one blow after another?' The blows come because we live in the psychological land of blows. We get what we get because we live where we live.

This book speaks frequently about changing our mental residence and about uplifting our level of being. You can see why. These actions take us out of the land of lightning.

LAW OF ATTRACTION

The simple wish to understand that which you do not at present understand is a powerful force. Release it fully. Let it work for you. That is the purpose of psychic energy — to revitalize you. So release it right now, whether working with others or all by yourself.

A husband and wife asked for and received an appointment with a teacher of real knowledge. The husband said, 'We wish to understand why certain things happen to us.'

The wife added, 'This will help us attract only those events which are worthwhile.'

The teacher explained, 'You attract whatever corresponds to your own nature. Like attracts like. This is natural law. Tigers associate with other tigers. Doves fly together. Change what you are and you will change what you attract. Self-change starts by seeing yourselves as you really are, not as you imagine you are. Work together with these ideas.'

LAY DOWN THE WEAPONS

Travellers during the Middle Ages found food and rest at various castles along the way. But a requirement was made for entrance. Anyone wishing to cross the drawbridge and enter the castle had to leave his weapons with the guard at the gate. No one could enter with hostile weapons such as swords and crossbows.

When hearing this illustrative story in class, Gary commented, 'The point is clear enough. We cannot carry weapons of antagonism and aggression into the castle of truth. I think that is one of our greatest problems. In the first place we are so unaware of how much hostility we have towards the very castle which offers relief from the long and weary road.'

'What we fail to see,' added Marilyn, 'is that weapons are unnecessary in the castle. To be inside means you have won, so what is there to fight?' Marilyn concluded, 'How to lay our weapons down — that is what it is all about.'

LEARN TO DISTINGUISH

We cannot gain true profit as long as we assume we are already making it. Take mechanical religion, which is tragic loss. Mechanical religion appears to provide comfort and security, while actually increasing anguish. Rituals, ceremonies, vain repetitions, trite preachments, are stiff prison bars. Living from such memorized acts is like freezing in the snow while insisting it is warm because yesterday's weather forecast said it would be warm. Truth frees a man from all this by revealing that mechanical religion has all of the words but none of the music.

Guidance in this area can be gained by consulting the following list regularly. We must distinguish between:

The mechanical and the conscious.
The theatrical and the real.
The forced and the spontaneous.
The memorized and the new.
The nervous and the relaxed.
The useless and the beneficial.

LECTURES

A man once attended a truth-lecture. On his way home he complained, 'That teacher is not clear.' But he returned for the second talk. When walking home he reflected, 'Perhaps it is my own mind that is not clear.' He went back for the third lecture. While returning home he smiled and affirmed, 'I see clearly that the teacher was clear all the time.'

A person is attracted to esoteric truths only when seeing something valuable in them.

He sees something valuable in them only when also seeing something valueless in himself.

He sees something valueless in himself only when he is utterly tired of playing the self-deceiving game.

The light is always trying to break through the wrappings around life. Are we consciously aiding the light's breakthrough, or are we unknowingly opposing it?

LESSON ABOUT CHANGE

A teacher asked his class, 'If unhappiness exists in your mind, do you try to change your neighbour?'

'No.'

'What do you change?'

'The mind.'

'If confusion exists in your emotions, do you try to change the social system?'

'No.'

'What do you change?'

'The emotions.'

Asked the teacher, 'What lesson am I trying to teach?'

A student volunteered, 'You are instructing us in the need to work in the right place. A person suffering from himself gains nothing but more anxiety by trying to change others. Unfortunately, blaming others for our grief is a hardened human habit. Only self-work can change the self.'

LET NATURE SUCCEED
Human beings belong to so many things — to clubs and to other people and to religions and philosophies. Ask yourself, 'From a higher viewpoint, do I really belong to anything?'

You and I do not belong to anyone or anything, nor does anything in the exterior world belong to us. You and I belong to ourselves, to our true nature, to our own essence. As awakened men know, this is true success. *'Great men are the true men, the men in whom Nature has succeeded.'* (Henri Frederic Amiel)

So, you see, you do not need anyone on your side. You yourself are all you need. No other human being can be on your side anyway, except as his awakened essence touches your essence. You need only your own kingdom within. This is not a state of isolation and loneliness. It is self-completion at last.

LEVEL OF UNDERSTANDING
When losing the way when driving on a trip we do not become angry at ourselves or others. We look at a map to discover just where we went wrong. That is also the right procedure when straying off the road of life. Find out where you went wrong by studying your psychic maps, then make correction. Nothing is simpler than that. The trouble is that we complicate things with pointless reactions. The psychic maps you are studying in this book will pull you towards simple and corrective reactions.

'As a step towards greater self-knowledge, you urge us to see how little we know about ourselves. How can this be done?'

'Realize that you express your level of understanding in everything you do and feel and say. Every man *lives* his level for he has nothing else to live. Now look at the results of living out of your level of understanding or misunderstanding. What has it given you? Contentment or regret? Command or worry? Once seeing your level, work to raise it, which will raise results.'

LIGHTS AHEAD

Picture a motorist whose car breaks down in a wilderness. As night falls, a furious storm batters the car. The motorist feels fairly safe, but also feels trapped. Peering through the storm he sights distant lights which promise safety and assistance. But his mind is divided. One part of it urges him to dare to reach the lights, but another part argues in favour of the comfort of the car. For a while, his mind fights between the two choices.

Finally, he realizes what must be done. He leaves the safety of the car and struggles towards the lights. Every time he falls he wishes he had stayed in the car, but there is no turning back. He battles forwards until finally reaching the lights and safety.

This illustrates a particular point in spiritual progress. When first choosing the lights of truth, everything seems to get worse instead of better. It is not really worse; it is an awakening awareness of how badly off we really were. *This is a state of honesty and health*. The lights are just ahead.

LIGHTS ALONG THE PATH

The one way to begin to work for yourself instead of for nothing is to see what it means to work for yourself.

A person who thinks there is no alternative to his surrounding pressures is simply thinking incorrectly.

A healthy person without opposition in himself does not have opposition outside himself.

The upward path consists of the daily revelation of something about yourself to yourself.

An independent searcher asks many questions, but accepts only those answers which make him think for himself.

When solving the mystery of time, you will be able to do right now what you used to think would take years.

A denial of what you want can build great nobility if you

permit it to banish the fear of not getting what you want.

You will never go wrong by considering any difficulty as only an absence of understanding, which study can correct.

LIVING TRUTH

A truth is understood only when it favourably influences what the individual does, what he is. He must not only know the truth with his mind, but must live it with his whole being. Everyone must guard against taking mental knowledge of the truth for living it out in daily behaviour. An honest glance at the actual inward condition is enough to prevent a mistake here. Speaking the phrases 'kindly attitudes' and 'mental health' is not the same as living with those qualities.

You want a way of life, not a pill to be taken when desperation dictates. You want a freely flowing day requiring no stops for pills. You don't want just the words; you want the lasting inspiration of the music.

LOFTY WORLD

There is a way to live in which we are not indebted to anyone. In this lofty world we do not anxiously seek comfort or support from anyone, nor do we fear the loss of any benefits at present received from others. This is that rare independence known by those who have endured the quest to the very end. They have freedom by understanding the true nature of freedom, they have command because they place what is true above what is sparkling.

Just to ask intelligent questions of ourselves opens the door a bit wider. We can ask, 'Which indicates dawning wisdom — to chase every attractive sight, or to realize how easily these attractive sights turn into trouble?' Or we might inquire, 'Which makes sense — to tensely and endlessly defend myself against hurt feelings, or to end hurt feelings altogether by understanding their false power?'

LOOK FOR THE LESSON

Look for the valuable lesson in every unpleasant experience. It is there. The very experience indicates a need for the lesson. You would not have the experience unless you needed the lesson. A man on the right side of a bridge does not stumble on that bridge. We stumble simply because we are still crossing. We take the next step across as soon as we have learned the present lesson. A lesson learned is out of the way.

We learn the lesson simply by not refusing it. Refusal can take a thousand forms, some obvious, some subtle. Defending a false position is refusal, as is an attempt to shift one's own responsibility on to others. Each of us must detect his or her particular refusals and refuse them.

Do you know people whose faces grow tight and hostile at the slightest criticism of their ways? They reject the lesson. Do you know others who never give thought to anything higher than a football? They are ignoring gold.

That is not our way. Not any more.

LOSS AND FEAR

'Please supply an example of unconscious and injurious inner division.'

'People often say the opposite of what they really feel. For instance, anyone needing to convince others of how important his day has been has had an empty day.'

'Many people seem to have knowledge of religion and psychology, yet their personal lives are empty. Why?'

'Because surface knowledge is not enough to change human nature. Everyone knows that violence breeds violence, but men still attack each other. A willingness to give up egotism must accompany knowledge.'

'Please say something about the fear of loss.'

'Become fully conscious of your fear of losing someone or something. Let the healing facts you have gathered go to work on that fear. Then, if and when the loss comes, fear will not come with it.'

LOVE TRUTH

Gordon, who had been a doctor for thirty years, spoke up during the discussion period of the class. 'Please show us,' he requested, 'where we are making a mistake in our plans for self-awakening. We can then work to correct it.'

'Have you ever noticed the strange pleasure gained by falling into wild emotions, as when arguing? Have you ever observed the peculiar enjoyment you find in feeling gloomy? Have the courage to give up the false pleasure of negative emotions. Cease to secretly cherish self-torture and you can never feel tortured. This requires constant progress in self-knowledge. You must honestly see how much you love your negative feelings. Then you must love truth more, which breaks the power of self-injury.'

MAINTAIN DEFINITE AIMS

It is important to keep yourself with definite aims all the time. Here is why. Suppose you make it your clear aim to not speak impulsively today. Later, you catch yourself making an impulsive remark. You are now aware that you did not keep your aim, and it is this awareness which is pure gold for you. If you made no aim you would not be aware of breaking it. Success or failure in keeping your aim is not the important point; awareness of yourself in action is what you are after. Your aim in life is not to win, but to watch, but watching *is* winning.

A student asked his teacher, 'What if an individual is unable to reach the source of help he needs, such as a class with a self-awakened teacher?'

The student heard, 'Both the class and the teacher are merely ideas in your mind. You are in class every second, whatever you do. Also, the teacher is always present, for the teacher is your own essence. The kingdom of heaven is within.'

MAKE CONNECTIONS

Imagine a schoolboy having the date of 1848 in his mind but who is unable to connect it with the historical event of that year. He searches his mind until seeing the connection between date and event — the discovery of gold in California.

That is how your psychic system expands its power. By connecting one fact with another, a third force appears — that of new understanding. So make connections. Fresh insight follows. Perhaps you know of your uncertainty towards life. That is one fact. Now remember what you have learned about uncertainty. Remember that it is held in place by antique notions, including the notion that you must follow society's definitions of success. Know that you need not follow the definitions which keep the very definers outwardly successful but inwardly terrified. That is a second fact. Feel the truth of both facts at once. Certainty will replace uncertainty. This new and real certainty is a supreme king who pleads with no one for anything.

MAKE UP YOUR MIND

Once and for all, make up your mind to change the kind of human being you are.

Make up your mind to no longer live within walls. This will arouse screaming protests from the inner slave-masters. They will not easily yield their power over you. Be encouraged by hearing these protests, for they are your first insights into the false power of the slave-masters. They get frightened quite easily, and you are beginning to frighten them.

Hypnotized human beings have no knowledge of these facts, for they have never questioned their walls. They lived within concealed resentment and terror. They may live like this, but you cannot. You have places to go.

Here is something to remember every day: Nothing can withstand the audacious intention, 'I refuse to let go until I understand what this is all about.'

MAN IS SELF-DIVIDED

Man yearns to get rid of his pains and yet loves his pains for they make him the centre of his own attention. He seeks help in finding himself and yet rejects help because his vanity will not admit his misery. He wants to succeed in public affairs and yet does not want to succeed for he dimly senses the emptiness of public praise.

His agonizing contradictions are the result of his dualism, of his inner split. In other words, there are two opposing forces within him, one dominating him one moment and the other taking him over the next moment. These forces cease to act as *opposing* forces when he stops choosing one side against another. For example, when fully realizing the folly of human praise he no longer chooses it, and is therefore free from the anxiety of not hearing applause.

Above his dualism is Oneness. Oneness must be his single aim.

MAN'S CHIEF PROBLEM

'From the viewpoint of higher thought, what is man's fundamental difficulty?'

'Man's chief problem is his mistaken belief that he possesses a separate identity, an individuality that is apart from the Universal Whole, from the All. This false identity is like putting on one costume after another until the person believes he consists of the costumes he wears and the roles he plays. These wrong beliefs put him into conflict with both himself and others, for every label has an opposing label. A man believes he must present an impressive appearance to others. He is now afraid he will not be impressive. Reality is above all such labels and divisions. A real man never needs to prove himself, therefore, he is always at ease.'

MARVELLOUS REVELATION

A crisis occurs when reality challenges unreality. A problem arises only when truth confronts a false human position. The challenged person usually runs away from the crisis, thus losing the opportunity for healing through the replacement of falsehood by truth. Reality aids the challenged person by urging, 'Do not run away. Stay right where you are. Look at your crisis until seeing that you are the very crisis itself, that your own state of mind is the precise difficulty. Do this and a marvellous revelation appears. You see that you are also your own solution.'

Assistance often comes from the right word at the right time. One agitated man was bluntly told, 'Stop bothering yourself.' Receptive to help, he took it as a needed lesson. Brief self-examination revealed himself as the author of his agitation, which lifted him one more step above his old ways.

MATURITY AND BEHAVIOUR

'We are urged to place spiritual matters first. What does this mean?'

'You can talk about Truth and then talk about bread, but you cannot talk about bread and then talk about Truth. Understand Truth and you will understand bread.'

'Why does talk about a united world remain only talk?'

'Division begins in an individual mind and spreads itself throughout the world. Now, where must non-division begin if we are to unite the world?'

'May we have a clue for judging a person's actual level of psychic maturity?'

'Never estimate his maturity when things are going well with him. Anyone can smile in a calm sea. Watch his behaviour during a small or large crisis. That is what he is really like.'

'I want to be happy.'

'There is a part of you perfectly capable of straightening out another part of you. That should make you permanently happy.'

MEADOW AND CANYON

A flock of sheep once lived in a grassy meadow which was watered by a winding mountain stream. The sheep were tended by an alert and considerate shepherd. Living close to a nature which blended with their own nature, the sheep passed their days in contentment.

But over the months the sheep grew careless towards themselves. Disobeying the shepherd's instructions, they wandered off into a dry and treeless canyon which was closed at the opposite end. After a few days of hardship they began to blame the shepherd for their unhappiness. Then came a second phase in their thinking. They hypnotized themselves into believing that the canyon was the grassy meadow and that the meadow was the dry canyon.

Aware of how they had deluded themselves, the shepherd urged the flock to return to the meadow where everything would be clear once more. But the suspicious sheep shouted,

'Ah! So that's your trick. You want this meadow for yourself!'

MECHANICAL THOUGHT

Watch how your mind operates. Awareness of mental movements is rewarding and fascinating. Notice how it rolls along by associations. Hear the word 'candy' and the mind associates the word with a pleasurable feeling, exclaiming, 'Candy tastes good! I want some!' Meet a person who once hurt our feelings and the reaction leaps up, 'Danger. Be careful.'

Associative thought is mechanical. It races forward all by itself, like a driverless truck hurtling down a steep street. It captures the individual without his knowledge, carrying him to unpleasant places. Personal difficulties can be traced back to the domination of the person by associative and mechanical thought. Take someone who declares, 'I must win over my rival.' He may wish to win an argument or a game or an election. He wishes to win — and even lose — because in either case he gets a false feeling of life, and he is still on the level where he loves fiery feelings. Now he is in conflict with himself and others — all because he was carried off by mechanical thought.

An understanding of the mind enables us to live consciously instead of mechanically.

MEDALS

A deeply dissatisfied man looked around for ways to change his fortunes. An interesting idea jumped out of his mind, so he went to work on it. He designed an impressive medal on which was printed HERO. When wearing it in public he was instantly applauded and honoured by everyone.

But the thrill soon wore off for the man; also he noticed that fewer and fewer people were being impressed by the medal. So he designed a new medal on which was printed SCHOLAR. To his great delight the admiring throngs returned to cheer the new identification.

But this attraction faded also, forcing the anxious man to create a third medal. On this one was printed the word

LEADER. When displaying it outdoors he was loudly acclaimed as a great commander.

But somehow the man sensed that at no time was he ever really a different kind of person. The medals had no power to cover his haunting dissatisfaction. So in his secret thoughts he asked over and over, 'What will *really* make me different?'

MENTAL HEALTH IN ACTION

Whoever plunges bravely into self-discovery may feel at first that he is worse off than before. He may sight negative traits, causing disappointment or even shock. This is because he sees for the first time various traits which controlled him without his knowledge. This surprise comes to every earnest seeker. It is normal and necessary.

It is also good news. It is genuine advancement. It is mental health in action, for it includes the curing medicine of honest self-facing. Nothing but good can ever come from these disturbing revelations, regardless of how it feels at the present. It is like the temporary awkwardness you feel when learning a new game. Your very awareness of incapacity becomes an incentive for winning capacity.

MENTAL IMPRISONMENT

It is precisely because an awakened man knows how the mass-mind operates that he does not talk to everyone about the way out of mental prison. Most people do not even realize they are imprisoned, so why listen to someone who talks about the way out? To whom does the enlightened man speak? To those who have peered beyond the pretty curtains to see the prison bars which have always confined them. Only prisoners who know they are prisoners are interested in escape plans. They are the ones who get out.

If you are ever fortunate enough to hear a public talk by someone who knows what he is talking about, do not think of yourself as part of the audience. Pay no attention to the attitudes and reactions of others. Let the speaker talk to you personally, individually, just as if you were chatting as good friends in your home. It is the personal touch which makes the personal healing.

MENTAL MAGIC

Gregory was never hesitant about asking questions in class. This helped other students who were too shy to speak up. One evening Gregory said, 'It is good news to hear that an awakened man thinks in an entirely different way from the rest of us. As you have pointed out, we always think in the same old mechanical ways without even being aware of how dull and repetitious we are. But what about the mental magic of a real man? How does he see things differently and clearly?

'Suppose he passes a stranger on the street who has a gloomy face and manner. One glance at that stranger reveals a thousand facts to the real man. He knows that gloom never exists in isolation, but must be accompanied by dozens of other negative traits, like a gang of hoodlums. Therefore the real man knows that the stranger lives from sour outlooks and accusing attitudes, that he entertains illusory hopes of a better future, that he nervously feels himself at the mercy of people and events. This mental magic can be practised endlessly by anyone who becomes a real person.'

METHOD FOR ADVANCEMENT

There is a simple but dynamic method by which anyone can advance swiftly. When sensing you are doing something right, do it with increased frequency and energy.

Today, when meeting a problem or crisis, deliberately and persistently make the choice to understand it, rather than fight it. Start by seeing how your own mental operations might have contributed to the problem. But place the wish to understand the condition before the wish to battle against it. Do the same thing tomorrow, but with increased force and energy. Increase your effort even more the next day. Nature has given you a vast reservoir of energy. Release this energy as a trickle at first, and it will turn into a controlled flood.

Find even a small area where you are doing something you sense is true and good. It might be the reading of accurate books or an attempt to think more from your own original mind. Do more of it.

METHODS OF TRUTH

While there is only One Truth, its methods of expression are endless. Like waves washing a rock, truths appear in various shapes and sizes, but all come from the same immense sea.

The spoken or written word is one variety, as when hearing, 'If you want a rich gift, desire no gifts from men.' Observation of human nature is another teacher. Right behaviour can be learned from those who behave badly, for you can also see that wrongness always produces a fearful face. A third teacher is personal defeat. Be sure to welcome what men call defeats as eagerly as you welcome what men call victories — if you wish the Victory.

But be alert. Accept no teaching just because it is either new or traditional or because relatives and friends believe it. All roads do *not* lead to God. Only the road built with direct and personal experience leads to where you really want to be.

MIND AND EMOTION

Your aim is to allow mind and emotion to flow as one, just as two streams come together to form a commanding river. Lack of this harmony results in baffling conflict. Sometimes it is a dishonest feeling which blocks union, as when forcing an appearance of enthusiasm over something the mind finds boring. At other times the mind may be the deceitful partner. A person may feel it wrong to take advantage of others, but an insecure mind disagrees. The self-split individual is left with self-reproach.

When Margaret heard these ideas in class she stated, 'I can never make up my mind about anything. What you said appears to be a solution. Can internal oneness abolish indecision?'

'Succeed in your aim to not be in conflict with yourself, then see whether the problem is still there.'

MIND-POWER

Let your mind prove its powers to you. Here is one way to

do this.

Locate a specific problem. Turn every ray of light you have upon it, whether few or many rays. Let them work for you. That makes the light grow brighter. Maybe you do not understand why so many things go wrong for you. But perhaps you are beginning to understand that things go wrong for invented personality, but never for your real nature. Now go on from there. Study sections in this book which explain the difference between artificial personality and your true self. The light will grow. And while walking in the light the usual unhappy events will no longer happen to you. They cease to happen because you now understand why they happened. They happened because you did not really realize you were walking in dark places. But now you know the difference between darkness and light, so there is no more stumbling.

MIRACULOUS SECRET

No human being has ever cried, 'What am I going to do?' without the answer being as close as his own willingness to hear it. What you wish to hear can be heard.

Does a certain part of you want to awaken from the human nightmare? If so, everything that happens to you is on the side of this yearning portion of your psychic system. Everything means everything, even conditions which seem to work against you. This is a strange but miraculous secret which few people ever discover. The next paragraph will let you in on the secret.

If only you will sense the power of disillusionment! Do so. Seek out and bring to light all the disillusionment you can find in yourself. Consciousness of shattered dreams is power and honesty and the beginning of the end of disillusionment. We can go nowhere without first seeing our dismay with successes which fail. We can go as far as we want by boldly entering the tunnel of disillusionment, for the entrance reveals the exit.

MISFORTUNE CAN END

'Some of us seem to attract trouble, especially trouble with other people. What must we see?'

'First see that many of your troubles are caused by associating with wrong people. Then you must see that something wrong in you attracts these people, for like attracts like. This is where strict self-examination and self-honesty come in.'

A misfortune truly understood does not repeat itself. Deeply understanding the cause, you no longer put it into motion, thus preventing the effect. The ability to stop self-damage before it happens is one of the wonders of the esoteric path. A person then sees how he could have stopped earlier misfortunes, had he been awake.

Many insights contribute to the whole understanding needed to prevent the repetition of misfortune. One insight is to see how the disaster was unconsciously invited by foolish desires. Many a man or woman wakes up after an unhappy involvement with the opposite sex to see the foolishness of his or her desires.

MISLEADING HOPE

There was once a wealthy nobleman who was able to purchase everything he wanted. He surrounded himself with the most beautiful women of the land, and he dined lavishly.

One day a series of events took away all that he had owned and cherished. When trying to recapture his former glory, he failed miserably. So he lived on hope, comforting himself, 'Someday I will be a great man again.' But his pain and fear grew so great he decided to consult a wise man.

'Relief will come,' counselled the wise man, 'only when you abandon all hope. Do you not see that your very hope is your anguish? You see, hope creates the illusion of self-division. To explain this, you falsely believe there is a self and something else which will rescue this self. This is illusion. Life is not divided like this, but hope makes it appear so. So cheerfully abandon hope. You will then see no need to be rescued from anything outside yourself. Your awareness of oneness is total rescue.'

MISTAKE AND CORRECTION

These principles expand an individual's capacity for thinking outside of himself. This unique way of thinking provides clear judgment in both inner matters and in external activities. The person possessing it enjoys an ease and efficiency not known by the self-enclosed man or woman.

We can examine a person unable to think outside of himself. So concerned is he with building and defending his fictitious self-images he has no real interest in anything else. In public he may appear to have tender concern for a troubled world, but that is simply one of his many deceptive schemes for preserving his flattering illusions about himself. He is imprisoned in his own mind.

The preceding paragraph provides a clue for the man who wants to work against that which works against him — self-enclosed thinking. He can become aware of how self-centred thoughts keep him exactly where he really does not wish to be — within the whirling wheel of nervousness and doubt. He can see how his mistake about himself has made his life the secret tragedy that it is. Then he can bravely and cheerfully set about correcting the mistake.

MOMENT OF LIGHT

One result of self-investigation is the feeling that here at last you have found that mysterious treasure that a certain part of you always wanted. This treasure comes to those with honest doubt about their goals in life.

At first a man does not know what to do with himself. He then chooses several goals, but finds them both elusive and contradictory. When selecting one of them as his main goal he still finds himself aimless and dissatisfied. Then, when having courage to see the emptiness of all his self-chosen goals, he experiences a strange kind of shock. This strange shock carries him to the truth at last. He realizes that the only real thing he has to do with himself is to find himself. At that moment of light all questions about earthly goals fade away. Because his ego is no longer active, he simply earns his living in any way he can, while devoting every possible minute to his Supreme Goal.

MORE LIGHT

Max came right to the point about his problem. 'Every night there is a new domestic crisis. Large or small, it is always there. What can be done with them?'

It was apparent that Max was still trying to solve the problem instead of solving himself. He was told, 'Working on the exterior expression of the problem is like trying to mop up the kitchen floor while leaving the tap running. You are the tap that spills water all over the floor. Turn it off.'

Max nodded with the comment, 'I suspect that is right, but I need more light. As you say, light is all we need.'

At times the guiding light ahead of you in the passage may seem to go out, but it is still there, reappearing as you turn the next corner in the twisting passage. Your part is to keep going until turning the corner.

MOVE TOWARDS OPEN SPACES

The move away from self-enclosure towards free and open spaces reveals itself at first in small ways. Take a person who accidentally receives a letter intended for a neighbour. Disappointed that it is not his own, he drops it with annoyance and hurries back to his habitual worries. The letter attracts his glance from time to time, causing unconscious guilt and conflict. After hours or days he may see that the letter reaches the neighbour, but feels resentful at having to do something which returns no reward.

But now he is a different kind of man with a mind operating in a truly positive way. Somewhere along the track he called a halt to the madness. A new set of responses has been acquired. Another misdirected letter arrives. One glance and his reaction is relaxed and correct. There is no battle, no waste of energy. Having burst the bag of self-centredness, he is able to put himself in his neighbour's place. Realizing how important the letter might be, it is returned promptly.

NATURAL LIVING

You can drive your car uphill for ten or fifty miles, but you know that sooner or later the road will turn downhill. You are sure of this because you understand the natural laws of geography. You realize that no car can travel uphill or downhill endlessly. They must alternate with each other.

Connect this with your daily course. The same law of alternation applies. The wise teachings of Taoism call it the law of *yang* and *yin*. Most people do not know this law. A person fails to casually enter the flow which alternates uphill and downhill. Instead, he identifies with uphill, that is, he falsely believes he can survive psychologically only if events match his acquired desires. So he fights ridiculously and vainly to make the road run uphill all the way.

But the natural man has an easy road all the way. He does not proceed while hoping for uphill and therefore worrying over downhill. He is not fighting for a fictitious survival. He is above that. He lives.

NATURALNESS AND ARTIFICIALITY

Knowledge comes first. Books and classes help here. Then we must live what we know. This is achieved by letting knowledge banish artificial life. Knowledge states, 'Most of what you do and say is a desperate attempt to make the mythical look real. And by the way, these artificialities you love so much are the very things you complain about, but you don't see your contradiction.' By welcoming this knowledge, by not fighting it, we permit its power to banish artificiality. So by losing imaginary life we live at last in real life.

Someone asked, 'How can knowledge lead to freedom and naturalness in human relations?'

'Simply *see*.'

'See what, for example?'

'That you are the slave of anyone you fear.'

'That supplies freedom?'

'Yes, for no man is ever knowingly enslaved.'

NAVIGATION

'I am tired of not being myself. What can be done?'

'There is just one way to start living from yourself. It is to detect and abolish the imaginary self which now controls your acts and words and feelings. This is why these classes emphasize the need to see through and drop artificial personality.'

'Why does anyone repeat self-punishing behaviour?'

'Because he fails to remember himself. He forgets what happened to him the last time he did what he did. His overpowering craving for pleasurable sensations blocks out awareness of the troubles he attracted the last time. He must become conscious of the whole picture.'

'Something is wrong with our daily navigation. How can we stay on course?'

'Here are two guides by which anyone can learn to navigate correctly. Whoever refuses the uncomfortable feeling of being wrong can never be right. Whoever endures the discomfort of feeling himself wrong will become right.'

NECESSARY ACTION

A lion was captured and placed in a large yard surrounded by a high fence. He soon became acquainted with the social life of the other lions who had been there a long time. The lions had divided themselves into several clubs, each with its own activities. One group met regularly to hate and slander the captors. Another group met to sing sentimentally about a future jungle having no fences. And a third group met to secretly plot violence against the other groups.

Each club tried to pressure the newcomer into joining, but something held him back. His hesitation was caused by observing one particular lion who kept to himself and who seemed to be in deep thought. The newcomer shyly approached the solitary lion and requested an explanation of his apartness.

'Join nothing,' replied the lion. 'Those foolish creatures do everything but the necessary. I am doing what is essential, so one day I will be out of here. You are welcome to all the facts I have uncovered.'

'But what is this necessary thing you are doing?'

'Listen carefully. *I am studying the nature of the fence.*'

NEGATIVE THOUGHTS AND FEELINGS

Remember these facts about negative thoughts and feelings. They clear up many puzzlements about human nature, revealing people as they really are. This insight gives you calm command in all human relationships.

The appearance of one negative word or act in a person indicates the existence of dozens of other negative characteristics. Here is what this means. When seeing an angry man, you also see someone with a depressed, worried and frightened nature. When observing a sour and scornful woman, you also observe a weak and tense woman. Negative characteristics are like a school of sharks. You may see only one at a time, but dozens of others are swimming below the surface.

Take these facts into consideration when entering any human relationship. Then, because you see all of the person standing before you, no one will ever be able to deceive you.

NEWNESS IN THE NOW

A good and thoughtful king offered a ride in his carriage to a weary traveller on the road. Having been treated badly by evil kings, the traveller hesitantly asked, 'Sir, what must I give in return?' The understanding king replied, 'Just one thing. Your acceptance of the offer.'

Let the answer to life be as acceptable as it is simple. You will travel fast! People endlessly ask, 'How can I feel well?' The only possible answer is, 'Be well.' But this arouses instant resistance, for it means we must turn away from old and habitual roads, and this frightens our old nature.

Don't let habit tell you what to do. Don't let the past control your thinking. Accept the offer of newness in the now. Just accept.

NEW RELATIONSHIPS

Marvin wanted to know, 'How does a changed attitude towards ourselves make change and refinement in our attitudes towards others?'

'When you no longer believe in your own psychic shipwreck, you no longer believe in the permanent shipwreck of others. This creates a new relationship with others. Among other victories, you are no longer bothered by their unwise or irritating behaviour. Having found inner liberty for yourself, you know it is possible for them also — if they want it deeply enough. You are like a man who makes it to shore after leaving a sinking ship. You sight others clinging to bits of the broken ship, knowing they can also reach the shore if only they will look in the right direction.'

NEW THINKING

An individual does not have dozens of problems. He has only one fundamental problem. Realizing this is like leaping over a high fence that blocked our path.

What is it?

It is the illusion that ordinary thinking can solve problems. Ordinary thought, conditioned thought, cannot solve problems because it is the very cause of problems. Habitual thinking, frozen thinking, cannot teach us anything new, any more than a polar bear can teach anything about tropical bananas. It is strange how we fail to see this. Furiously and frantically, we battle for years in an attempt to think our way out, but new walls appear at every turn.

A totally new way of thinking is required. This thinking

does not look to conditioned memory for an answer. Instead, the mind waits quietly for something higher than memory to speak. The resulting answer solves all problems.

NEW VIEW

Suppose you are on the third floor of a ten-story building. You have never gone above this level. Then you meet someone from the tenth floor who describes the higher view from up there. You may have difficulty understanding what he is talking about. Then you ascend to the tenth floor and look out of the window. Your own vision reveals what it is all about.

All our questions are finally answered. Most answers turn out to be utterly different from what our habitual thinking imagined they would be. We may have wondered why esotericism says so little about comfort and sympathy. We see why. It is because there is something a thousand times better than comfort. It is the disturbing but liberating truth about ourselves. We may have been puzzled at the endless repetition of troubles. We solve the mystery. We caused our own problems by not seeing the difference between mechanical thinking and higher perception.

NOBLE COURAGE

Ralph spoke up for the entire class. 'We have given ourselves the project of ending wrong reactions. Please give us a place to work.'

'Have you ever observed the resulting thrill when someone says he likes or appreciates you? Do not respond wrongly to that feeling. You may assume it tells you who you are, for example, that you are indeed a friendly and worthy person. You have wrongly let that feeling reinforce your flattering self-images. Instead of falling victim to false reactions, let them fall on your wish to understand what they are all about. Try to see how you believe what you prefer to believe, how you choose the elation of flattery over facing your actual condition. That is noble courage.'

NOBLE NECESSITY

An apple seed found itself resting on the shady side of a large rock. It felt comfortable and secure in its familiar surroundings. One morning a swift wind suddenly picked up the seed and carried it away. After whirling round strange skies for a while, the seed came down in a field of rich earth.

At first the seed felt frightened and insecure. While yearning for its former familiar surroundings, it wondered why the wind had treated it so harshly.

Then the seed noticed something about itself. It saw that it was changing, growing, becoming something far greater than it had been before.

Finally, the seed understood what had happened to it. It saw the noble necessity for leaving the old place to enter this new land of greater development. It also realized that the wind was a friendly force after all.

NON-ACTION

For a while, instead of thinking of things you must do for self-progress, think of what you must not do. We can see what is involved here. A person usually has a long mental list of actions he wants to take, but forgets that not-doing is also a form of doing. In fact, esoteric non-action is a special kind of creative action.

Think about it. How would a man's day be different if he did not try to force his way through it? By not forcing anything he would avoid the tension and strife that always accompanies forcing. Forcing falls away when we clearly see it as a wrong move. We need only be conscious that anything gained by either subtle or violent force becomes just another chain.

Go into non-action.

NON-INTERFERENCE

A seeker asked, 'What do I fear?'

'You fear to dismiss *your* answer, for you believe there may be no other answer to replace it. You would rather be wrong than empty. This fear terrorizes most people. I will help you. Dismiss *your* answer. Let the emptiness be there. Remain right in the centre of it with an awareness of how it shakes you. Then, someday, you may return here. When meeting, we will not need to say a word; we will just smile at each other.'

Whole Life is perfectly capable of answering every question, providing our habitual nature does not try to help. An attempt to help only interferes with the natural revelation. It is like pushing on a walking man in an attempt to help him move forward.

The mind asking the question cannot answer it. Only a higher mind can do so, which requires that we cease to push this way and that in an attempt to move towards an answer. So stay clear. Do not interfere. This is the great secret taught by Taoism. Let Whole Life do what it knows how to do.

NOTHING PREVENTS YOU

Entering the classroom, a teacher wrote five separate sentences on the blackboard.

Nothing prevents you from comprehending everything you need to comprehend.

Nothing stands in the way of your possession of a carefree spirit.

Nothing blocks your ability to end a mistake-making way of life.

Nothing obstructs your view of the kingdom you have always wanted to inherit.

Nothing prevents you from attaining a calm confidence that no wordly event can shake.

After studying the blackboard for a while, a student asked the teacher, 'What prevents us from understanding these messages?'

'Nothing prevents you from understanding these messages.'

OBSERVE OTHER PEOPLE

As a personal project, look behind the physical appearance of another person to penetrate the secrets of the inner man. Ignoring his physical self for the moment, try to see the psychological person who stands before you. Be aware of why he says what he does, notice how easily he is distracted by a sudden noise, observe tension or irritation in his general manner.

After practising this for a while you may be astonished at how the observed person seems to change before your eyes. He is not what you thought he was. The person whom you thought you understood has become a stranger who is far less confident than he appeared to be. Of course, the person has not changed at all. You are seeing him as he really is behind his external stage performance.

The purpose of this practice is not to criticize the other person, but to see his actual condition, to know the psychological person. This works for you in many ways, including the talent for independence in human relations.

OCCUPY YOURSELF

'About three years ago,' said Milton, 'a strange restlessness possessed me. Its very vagueness was frightening. I felt urged to search for something, but had no idea what it might be. All I knew was that I could not continue with my usual life. Am I making sense?'

'Perfect sense. Consciousness of restlessness is the first stirring of new life. Your next step is to give direction to this restlessness, for it contains great energy.'

'But I need so much help. Is it available?'

'You can have all the help you want providing you want help more than you want anything else.'

'Something is happening to me. What is it?'

'What is happening is that your world is becoming too small for you. You said you cannot go on with your usual ways. That is tremendous. Already you are bursting out of boundaries. Now, occupy yourself with these teachings until they tell their full and fascinating story.'

OFFICE BUILDING

Picture a ten-story office building. Businessman A occupies an office on the first floor, as does Businessman B. The first floor is a madhouse of confusion where papers get lost and contradictory orders are given. Weary of the chaos, Businessman A moves up to the second floor where he finds conditions somewhat better. Pleased, he sends a message down to the first floor, informing Businessman B of the improvement. But B fails to investigate, besides, he does not believe A.

The encouraged Businessman A next moves to the third floor which proves to be even better than the second floor. Once more he contacts B, but B finds the second message even more unbelievable than the first. So Businessman A continues to move upwards into better and better conditions, but B remains on the level of chaos.

Businessman A is an example of what can happen to anyone who no longer wants chaos. He knows that his success can also be the success of others.

But will they listen?

ONE MIND

Practise putting yourself in the other person's place. It is a highly scientific method for self-liberation, which is the same as self-contentment. Swinging over to the other's viewpoint serves as a hammer for knocking down the illusory wall between the individual and the universal whole. As the wall crumbles, so do anxious strivings, for now there are no enemies or competitors to conquer.

The practice is easy enough. Just try to see everything from his viewpoint, which does not require agreement. The point is to see both his side and yours at the same moment, which produces an astonishing result. You realize that where there are opposite positions, true co-operation among men is impossible. After that an even more astonishing light glows. You have transcended dualistic thinking. You are above the tyranny of self-concern because you are above the synthetic self which operates with double thinking. Your mind is One.

ONENESS

What is the nature of this new world we are exploring together? It is totally unlike anything you have ever experienced before. It exists within you, a magnificent world, unseen by the five senses, but felt by those psychic faculties attuned to it. It is a world of authentic self-command. You see, everyone knows there is something missing from his life, but does not know what it is. What is missing is Oneness.

We do not, in fact, lack Oneness. We *are* Oneness. The damage is done by lack of realization. That is why humanity is like a group of frantic people who think they must run on the riverbank alongside the boat, instead of riding in it. You are learning to ride.

ONE OBJECTIVE

These studies are all about the solving of daily problems, the ending of unwanted experiences, the winning of self-command. They show us how to fight for, not against, ourselves.

Certainly we must fight for ourselves, but must understand what it means to battle for self-victory. The spiritual battle must include no negative aims, such as the wish to attract attention or the desire to feel superior to others. Such aims always end in despairing defeat, for they are vain attempts to pin medals on to a non-existent person. There is no such thing as a separate self which can attract attention or win over supposed rivals.

The spiritual soldier marches towards one objective only. He aims to win over his own warring illusions. He wishes to stop being his own worst enemy.

OPEN MIND

Consider your problem, whatever it might be. Perhaps it involves marriage or finances or health. Or perhaps you fear losing your security, or maybe you cannot obtain what you feel you must have.

Next, remember that there is a great difference between thinking about a problem and having a completely open mind towards it. Thinking about a difficulty cannot end it because the thought and the difficulty reside on the same psychological level. Conditioned thought is the very cause of the problem, therefore it cannot save itself. Something higher is needed. This something higher exists within a truly open mind, a mind which neither attacks nor defends a problem. An open mind ends the illusion of an individual self, which ends the illusion of a problem-burdened person, which ends the illusory existence of the problem.

Have an open mind towards the preceding paragraph.

OPERATION OF COSMIC LAW

Ponder the cosmic principle, 'Whatever you wish for another, you also wish for yourself.' This applies to every person, whether or not he is aware of it.

Read it again. 'Whatever you wish for another, you also wish for yourself.' It cannot be otherwise. Look how it proceeds with a negative wish. Tom has been hurt by Bill, so he takes mental revenge by wishing misfortune towards Bill. When Tom wishes misfortune towards Bill it plainly indicates that Tom himself lives in a house of misfortune, for Tom can give out only what he has for himself. So each time Tom secretly wishes misfortune for anyone, he has no choice but to wish it for himself. He is his own wish, and is therefore his own punishment.

To break this dismal pattern, Tom must become conscious

of how this cosmic law operates. It will then swing over to its positive side. By living in his own recovered light, Tom will naturally wish this abundant light for others.

OPPORTUNITY FOR SELF-CHANGE

'Many people fear the rescuing facts. Why?'

'Truth always seems harsh and frightening to an unwise hearer. This is because he plays his usual game of seeing the truth as *he* is, not as truth is. Everyone has an opportunity for self-change by letting the truth be whatever it wants to be.'

'Please review your statements about giving to others, about generosity. There is considerable confusion here.'

'A person has only one thing to give to others — his own level of maturity or immaturity. That is the whole story. So who is the truly generous person? Obviously, the one who actively seeks to raise his own level of cosmic maturity.'

'You hit the target with me at the last meeting. You said we exhaust ourselves in needless efforts to prove ourselves right.'

'There is only one way to prove yourself right, which is to never try to prove it. Real rightness has no need to prove itself any more than an eagle needs to prove he is one.'

OPPOSING SIDES

A man who takes a side can never know the truth. Truth is above all man-made sides and positions. Where there is Side A there must be Side B, which creates conflict. Truth has nothing to do with conflict. This cosmic principle frightens immature thinkers, for they take sides in order to gain feelings of importance and individualism. They fight back by asking, 'How can life go on unless we develop opposing sides? We can then select the features from both sides which we believe best.' That is typical delusion. God, Truth, Reality, does not have to believe anything. Reality *knows*. Besides, it might be asked, 'Honestly, now, what is man's condition under his present method of taking sides?'

It takes great courage to let go of sides. It means one must no longer live by the labels which seemed to provide satisfaction and security. It means the end of the false pleasure of battling with the opposite side.

But above the opposites is the Real.

ORATORS

A man was travelling through the wilderness when he came across some animals having a speech contest. The judge was a lion who invited the man to become part of the audience. The man accepted.

A fox stood up and gave a smooth and clever speech. At one point he declared, 'The moon is larger than the sun.'

The next speaker was an elephant whose voice boomed out with power and authority. His talk included the sentence, 'Summer is colder than winter.'

Then came a tiger whose eloquence impressed everyone. At one point he said, 'The river runs uphill.'

The observing man remarked to the lion, 'They are superb orators. However, I am puzzled. All of them made statements which were obviously untrue. Not only that but the audience either did not notice or did not care. Why do your speakers make false statements?'

'That is an unworthy habit all right,' admitted the lion, 'but the audience is more interested in entertainment than enlightenment. I have often wondered where we picked up the habit.'

ORIGINAL PLACE

Luther Burbank, the botanical genius, presented hundreds of new varieties of fruits and vegetables to the world. He had a simple method for testing a new fruit he believed was particularly flavoursome. Asking his friends to close their eyes, he gave them a slice of the new fruit. Their reactions to the new taste supplied helpful information to Burbank. Since it was a new fruit, the friends had to react from an original place within themselves, not from mere memories of other fruits they had eaten.

Each person has an original place within himself,

untouched and uninfluenced by past experiences. It may be unfound as yet, but it is there. This original place is totally self-governing, depending upon nothing outside itself. It knows instantly the difference between the taste of truth and what conditioned memory labels as the truth. It knows what is truly right for itself, receiving that alone, declining all else.

Whoever lives from his original place receives its unique refreshment all day long.

OUTDOOR CLASS

It was a pleasant day, so a teacher and his audience were having an outdoor session. Since the audience was large, the teacher used a microphone. In the middle of the talk the sound system broke down. The teacher used the opportunity to teach a lesson. Offering the microphone to the nearest man, the teacher requested, 'Will you make this right?'

The man explained as he shook his head, 'I'm sorry, but I do not understand sound systems.' The microphone was offered to several others, but each explained his inability to repair it.

'Ah!' the teacher applied the lesson. 'You cannot repair the microphone because you do not understand it. Yet you expect to stop feeling lonely without understanding what loneliness is all about. You wish to conquer anxiety without seeing into the nature of anxiety.'

The audience nodded in understanding of the lesson.

OVER THE BRIDGE

There is a particular bridge along the cosmic trail which can be crossed with elevated understanding. The bridge appears when a newcomer asks questions such as, 'How can I solve my financial problems?' and, 'What can I do about a troublesome relative?' The teacher's answer may seem ir-relevant; he may appear to be discussing something entirely foreign to the question. The teacher might reply, 'Wisdom towards finances must follow wisdom towards your own mind,' or, 'Is there an unseen part of you which secretly enjoys having trouble with this relative?' Bewildered and disappointed, the inquirer feels that the teacher cannot help.

What happens, of course, is that the beginner makes the mistake made by all beginners. He expects the answer to be on the same level as the question. He cannot as yet conceive a solution which is beyond conditioned thought. So though hesitant at this bridge, he can study it until perception enables him to cross over.

OVERWHELMING CIRCUMSTANCES

Lucy asked, 'What can we do when feeling overwhelmed by circumstances?'

'Any time you feel the walls are closing in on you a simple remedy is on hand. Just see where the walls exist — in your own mind and nowhere else. Let them overwhelm you and they will disappear.'

'I would like to understand that last sentence.'

'A certain part of the mind operates incorrectly, thus creating the illusion of walls. These walls cannot exist unless given life by another part of the mind *which creates them by fighting them*. An illusion is conquered by not fighting it, by sitting aside and calmly watching its strange antics.'

'Why is watchfulness so effective?'

'Because it calls the bluff on illusion. You see, illusion has no power in itself. It depends entirely upon the careless co-operation of the person it attacks. When you calmly observe it instead of fighting back it gets discouraged and goes away in defeat.'

PATIENCE

Patience is a virtue in our inner endeavours. Be patient. Do not be impulsive. When you do not know what to do, do something different. Do not anxiously plan. Do not demand an answer. Do not run somewhere.

Stay where you are. Be calm. Wait. But wait actively. Reflect about your life here on earth. Read an informative book. Discuss with others. Learn the movements and motives of your own mind.

The answer will come. But it will not be the answer you expected. What you expected was either a 'yes' or a 'no'. Your answer will be neither of these, for it is above all such expected opposites. It is *the* answer, not an unconsciously *desired* answer.

Stay where you are. That changes where you are. You elevate yourself to a lofty position which clearly reveals the answer, like a man on top of a wall who sees both sides at once. From this height you realize that the answer to the question consists of the very disappearance of the question. A man on top of a wall has no questions as to what is on either side. He sees, knows, rests.

PEARLS

A student of truth asked his teacher, 'Why do so many people continue with error instead of finding truth?'

Replied the teacher, 'Because error is like leaves scattered on the surface of the sea. They are easy to collect. Truth is like pearls in deep water. Few men care to take the adventurous dive. Be one of the adventurers.'

Adventure with this thought. You can do as much as you can see — if you really know what it means to see. To the undivided man, seeing and doing are the same thing. To *do*, *see*.

See this: You are living in the real world when you don't care whether or not it collapses. However, this real world can never collapse. Only a false world can do that. Those living in the real world know all this. For this reason the notions of collapse or non-collapse have no place in their minds. There is nothing to think about.

PERSISTENT PROBLEMS

'There are so many new problems every minute,' commented Roy. 'It seems impossible to even begin to handle them.'

Roy and the class were told, 'In one sense, no one ever has new problems. He has new forms of his old problem, which is lack of self-knowledge. A troubled man hacks vainly at sour fruits, leaving the unhealthy roots to continue their work. Take the problem of self-rejection, which creates other problems, including depression and a frantic search for approval. The whole problem vanishes by understanding that the rejected self has no real existence. It is merely a dream-picture, a false idea one has about oneself, an unconsciously-played stage role. Suppose an actor plays the role of a persecuted man. What happens to his persecution when he walks offstage?'

PERSONAL COMMUNICATION

In early civilization, long-distance communication was achieved with waved flags, smoke signals, reflections in a mirror. Effectiveness was limited, for hills and groves could block visual contact. Inventors and scientists developed the telephone and radio and television which leaped mountains with ease.

As an esoteric scientist, you are developing new methods for communicating with inner forces. One of them is the realization that whatever is wrong for you is also unnecessary. Consider this tremendous fact. It means you need not cringe before anyone or anything. Fear is always wrong, so it is completely unnecessary. Whether realized or not, this is a fact. Realize it for yourself.

You can develop direct and effective communication with your inner forces.

PERSONALITY CLASH

Requested Elizabeth, 'Please explain what is commonly called a personality clash between two people.'

'It involves two confused people who hope to win the argument while fearing to lose. They hope to win in order to confirm the pleasant pictures they have of themselves, such as being intelligent or authoritative. But you can't confirm illusions, so the battle is in vain. A free man never has such clashes, for he has no need to prove anything. He lives above mental self-portraits. If someone behaves angrily towards a free man, it means nothing to him.'

Asked Elizabeth, 'Why not?'

'Anger hurts only when it strikes the false self in the intended target. A free man has no false self.'

PIECES OF GOLD

Eric commented, 'I am sure there are many lessons we will learn which we don't even suspect at the present time. Some of them may even shock us, as have some of our past lessons. Will you please prepare us for one of them?'

'You may think that a certain person cares for you. As happens with many people, you may see he never really cared for you at all, but merely used you for selfish purposes. Your beautiful dream is shattered. You may feel with rage and shame that the other person made a fool of you. Go beyond that useless emotionalism. Examine the shattered pieces of the dream. They are pieces of gold. See that you were asleep, otherwise you would not have had a dream to be shattered. See that you don't need deceptive dreams. See that you have been shocked — but shocked awake. Now stay awake to prevent it from happening again. What superb progress you are making!'

PLEASANT ATMOSPHERES

'Will you please discuss psychological atmosphere? For example, what makes us feel the way we do?'

'Every person is his own atmosphere. To state it another way, we *feel* what we *are*. How can it be otherwise? So in order to dwell in more pleasant atmospheres we must transform the nature which causes them. A cherry tree feels the nature of a cherry tree because that is the only nature it has. So it is with us. We can begin to see the truth of this by not depending upon exterior circumstances for happiness. Do you know why a cherry tree is naturally content? Because it is not trying to become an oak or a sycamore, but is content to be itself.'

'How can I be myself?'

'You are never anything but yourself. But this is hidden from you at present by artificial behaviour which strains to become a successful self or a popular self. By doing nothing to become someone you become yourself. Does a cherry tree try to become a cherry tree?'

POINTS TO PONDER

A man's level of psychic health consists of what he actually values, not what he says he values.

The aim of a chained man is to chain others, while the aim of a free man is to free others.

To 'let go' means to release conditioned thought because you see it is incapable of doing the work of consciousness.

A man in a state of psychic hypnosis does not know he dwells in psychic dreamland — and that is the entire human problem.

When living from truth, there is no compulsive need to defend it, for only unlived truth arouses compulsive defence.

When you do not know what to do about a crisis, remember that a quiet mind knows the whole answer.

The next time you meet what you call defeat, just stand there and be completely defeated — and watch what happens.

POSITIVE FUELS

At the start of each day an individual has his choice of two kinds of fuel. Whether his day is pleasant or not depends upon his choice. Many people actually depend upon the fuel of disturbance and irritation to carry them through. As strange as it sounds, they look forward to incidents which provide an excuse for emotional upset. This is because negative fuels provide a false feeling of life. The person feels alive and thrilled only when expending his negative fuels. He has the feeling of going somewhere, but it is illusory progress. He is merely agitating in a fixed position, like a factory machine.

But there are positive fuels which carry us forward as swiftly as they are employed. A few of them are watchfulness, inquiry, experimentation, daring. There is one fuel with extraordinary power. It is an ardent love for self-knowledge.

PRACTICAL ACTIVITIES

We must remind ourselves often of the need to separate practical activities from useless ones. A genuine teacher helps here, for he urges his listeners towards serviceable accomplishments only. Among other encouragements he urges people to:

Study and understand cosmic laws.
Free themselves from borrowed ideas.
Not refuse the lesson in heartache.
Awaken from illusions of being happy.
Not be afraid of themselves.
Decline to be influenced by other people.
Detect and end self-damage.
Deeply examine their inner condition.
Recognize and abandon worthless goals.
Devote cheerful energy towards self-change.

Select one of these for today's consideration. See it as a practical teaching which is on your side.

PREPARE YOURSELF

There is an interesting story about the introduction of dates from Egypt to the southwestern United States. Many years ago, agriculturists imported date palms, but because conditions were not right they failed to thrive. Scientific studies of the tree revealed the preparations which had to be made for successful date harvests. In addition to a desert climate, the date palm required extraordinary amounts of water. When preparations were complete, thousands of offshoots were imported from Egypt and Algeria. Date-growing now thrives in the United States.

Likewise, we need only prepare ourselves to make internal conditions ready. Then, like honoured guests, fresh truths enter and blossom all by themselves, refreshing us. Everything in this book contributes to your preparation.

PRESENCE OF MIND

The common saying 'He was absent-minded' conceals an uncommonly valuable lesson. In few words it describes man's woeful wandering and hints at the homeward course.

A negative response to an exterior challenge separates us from it, blocking comprehension. Anger or fear makes us absent from clear vision, and therefore prevents right action.

The opposite of absence is presence. So we can see what it means to maintain presence of mind. It means to keep your mind where the action is, to be fully aware of what you are doing at the moment you do it. This consciousness prevents negative reactions from separating you from the challenge. Staying at home with your own mind supplies a comprehension which never permits a challenge to become a problem.

Go home. Stay at home. There is rest.

PRINCIPLE OF SELF-CORRECTION

A troubled man starts rightly by thinking he needs rescue from something, but then makes a mistake. He believes he needs rescue from something other than himself. For example, being disappointed with his usual friends, he considers finding new people with whom to keep company. But he rarely considers the kind of thoughts with which he keeps company.

The man who stumbles with his mind has no choice but to also stumble with his foot. It is elementary psychological law that the foot must follow the mind. That is a simple and clear explanation of how the inner state reproduces itself outwardly, for either pain or peace.

Return every day to the principle of self-correction.

PROBLEMS

Esotericism is like a powerful flashlight. One beam of its light can plunge into the darkness, revealing shadowy figures to be nothing but harmlessly swaying trees.

Take the person who fears other people, a common and an unnecessary condition. That person lives under tyranny because of his own mental hypnosis. The problem resides in his own false beliefs about the power of other people.

False beliefs exist only in one's own mind. If the mind did not misunderstand, where would the belief exist? It would not exist at all. That is why your first thought upon arising in the morning should be, 'Well, what new insight can I win today?'

PROCEED WITH CONFIDENCE

Esotericism gets right to the point with perfect logic. Here is an example: 'If you are not the person you think you are you do not have the problems you think you have. You are not the person you think you are. You do not have the problems you think you have.'

Proceed with confidence in your ability to see what this means. Your confidence is rightly invested, for it is quite possible to grasp that which may presently seem beyond your reach. Just keep reaching. There is a certain realization which supplies strength for doing this. Realize the profound message in the next paragraph.

Truth alone is genuinely compassionate. All else is deception and exploitation. Living within the compassion of truth comes by examining both truth and deception until seeing the difference in the two. Remember, deception and exploitation cunningly masquerade as compassion. Look into your real nature, for it knows the difference in the two.

PROFITABLE QUESTIONS
A teacher of higher truth urged his students to ask profitable questions. When the students requested examples, the teacher said, 'Any question asked with a sincere wish for more light is a valuable question. You might ask how false assumptions can be banished. The answer is to see that false assumptions produce false happiness. You might want to know how to inspire your efforts at self-elevation. The answer is to see the happy necessity for self-elevation.'

Comprehension comes. It is like sitting before a window at daybreak, watching dark and vague shapes turn into recognizable trees and walls.

Remember that knowledge is a necessary acquisition, but that it is not the same thing as comprehension. We can read and remember a thousand books about rubies without ever seeing or holding a single ruby. Knowledge begins to turn into insight as we permit the facts to work on us, to alter attitudes and ideas.

PROFOUND LESSON
'I am unable to determine what is really beneficial for me.'

'You can know what is right for you only when knowing the difference between the artificial you and the real you. See the difference, otherwise you will wearily try to get something for a non-existent person.'

'Why do we get what we get?'

'You get always and only a return of your own nature. Whatever you *are* today, you *get* tomorrow. If you do not like what you get, change what you are.'

'Thanks to these teachings, I am beginning to see the perils of carelessly following those who are supposed to have the answers.'

'Yes. Like the owner of a café who dines somewhere else, many advisers would be horrified if they had to take their own advice.'

'All of us in this class know we have many elementary

lessons to learn. However, to make us think more energetically, may we have an especially profound lesson?'

'When you are at the complete mercy of everyone and
everything, and you do not fight, you have won.'

PROTECTION

Why does mankind fail to reach the other shore? Because a
man under the illusion of owning a yacht cannot be
persuaded to take lessons in rowing.

Here is a rowing lesson for those who want the other
shore: It is much easier to ask questions than to listen to
answers. Have you ever thought of that? For a while, reverse
the procedure. Instead of concentrating on questions, listen
with full attention to answers. Listen as if much depends
upon it, for it does. Listen to what the next paragraph has to
say.

The esoteric pioneer collects protective insights. One of
them is an understanding of how some people operate when
meeting others for the first time. Suppose a new person
comes into your life. Observe. He may subtly test the limits
of his liberties with you. Wanting something from you, he
will see how far he can go towards getting it without being
rebuked or stopped. Don't let him go anywhere. Be awake.
See through the game. Awareness is protection.

PSYCHIC HYPNOSIS

Gerald opened the class discussion with, 'We are told to
replace self-condemnation with self-understanding. I can see
how self-condemnation keeps us in the very self-centred trap
we wish to break. However, it is still necessary to examine
our blunders and contradictions. How can we look at
ourselves without falling into condemnation or guilt?'

'First of all, see that self-blame is just another mechanical
reaction which must be broken. Secondly, refuse to enjoy the
attention arising from self-condemnation, for attention promotes self-centredness. Thirdly, instead of labelling yourself
as evil or bad, see yourself as being under psychic hypnosis.
What we commonly call badness is the same as being in

psychic hypnosis.'

PSYCHOLOGICAL EARPLUGS

An incompetent carpenter once built a creaky house for himself, and maintained it as carelessly. The roof threatened to collapse; the floors were rough to walk upon. His neighbours warned him of the dangers and the unattractiveness of his house, but he angrily refused to listen. Finally getting tired of unwanted advice, he placed plugs in his ears. The warnings continued, but the carpenter only smiled, not hearing a word.

Inevitably, one day his house collapsed. Fortunately, the man escaped with only minor injuries. His neighbours scolded, 'See? We warned you. You are punished by your own stubbornness.' The carpenter just smiled pleasantly. He still wore his earplugs.

Incredibly, in spite of the disaster, the carpenter went right back to the same foolishness. He built and lived in another hazardous house. He was again warned, but never changed his perilous ways. That was because he had by this time taken his earplugs as both a normal and easy way of life.

This explains the tragic life of men and women who insist upon wearing psychological earplugs.

PSYCHOLOGICAL FUTURE

Anyone's psychological future can be predicted with absolute accuracy. Take a person who gets hurt by involvements with deceitful people who exploit and desert him. You might ask the injured person, 'Why did you get involved in that circumstance in the first place?' He may answer, but he will not really know why he walked straight into his own distress. This is because he fails to understand his mechanical desires. He is an unconscious human being — but not in a thousand years will you convince him of that. His future is certain. He will continue to stumble into trouble. Only the exterior scenery will be different.

Only one force can break the miserable pattern — a conscious way of life. He could listen earnestly to the question, 'Why did you get involved in that circumstance in the first place?' That will change the man, which will change his future, for he is his own future.

PSYCHOLOGICAL SLAVERY

'I now know what you mean by psychological slavery,' stated Louise. 'I fear people. Everyone seems so much more intelligent and authoritative that I spend most of my time cringing.'

'The only slave-master is your own conditioning. You must see how earlier hurts from people hardened into unconscious whips. Feeling inferior, you yourself project the illusion of their power and superiority. No one can hurt you *now*, but you live in memory, not in now. The next time you are with someone who appears strong and dominating, watch him carefully. Notice his nervous gestures, mechanical smiles, sudden blockages in thought and speech. You attribute power to him? Stop it at once! He is a weak and scared human being who has mastered the art of pretending. Nothing more. See this for yourself. Other insights must come, but start with this.'

PSYCHOLOGICAL SUNSHINE

There is a psychological law with enough sunshine to cheer up the most gloomy and defeated person on earth. Here it is: *No man knowingly works against his own true nature.* Before reading on, review that sentence. Even a glimpse of its significance can start your life on the upward path.

The word 'knowingly' deserves special attention. Any action taken against ourselves is performed unconsciously. Because we have not studied ourselves we do not see how we step on our own toes. As a simple example, Mr A puts pressure on Mr B, perhaps socially, politically, religiously, in office or home. The very wish to apply pressure is Mr A's own punishment, for no one can hurt another without already having that hurt within himself.

Since it is psychic sleep that makes us work against ourselves, the solution is obvious. We must wake up. It is the

awakening of self-knowledge that does the work for us.
From now on, be on your own side.

QUAKING MIND
In the morning a person puts some personal or business plan into operation while wondering, 'Is this the way life works?' At the end of a day of defeat he gloomily concludes, 'No, that is not the way it works.' His terror consists of not knowing which way to turn. His error consists of failure to see that his unenlightened nature can never know what to do. His quaking mind always thinks in terms of 'gain this' and 'avoid that'. He never sees that these attitudes contain terror and confusion in themselves. He needs to be told about a new kind of mind which commands every situation by not caring whether it commands it or not. In this enlightenment he will know how life works, which places him in true command of the beginning and ending of his day.

If we want to see something for ourselves we must do something for ourselves. We can either sit on the ground and peer through a crack in the fence or we can climb the fence and see everything on the other side.

QUALIFY YOURSELF
The need to 'let go' is so fundamental to the inner adventure you should remind yourself of it often. Just realize the necessity of abandoning whatever does no good, such as painful memories. Who would refuse to do that? It is a startling thought, but can you imagine anyone refusing to drop the useless and the burdensome? Man refuses. We know why. His peculiar logic takes the useless as a necessary item for survival. He rarely asks, 'But what kind of survival is it?'

He just sits and suffers from his peculiar logic.

An athlete wishing to win the game must qualify himself by abandoning activities which interfere with his performance on the field. Qualify yourself for self-conquest by letting go of whatever you sense must be dropped, perhaps resistance to a guiding fact.

QUALITY IN HUMAN RELATIONS

Attitudes towards other people are causes which produce the kind of effects we have in human relations. The attitudes we have towards others will be the same as those we have towards ourselves. Self-dislike must project itself outwardly in dislike of others, though pretence may conceal it. It is the actual attitude which hurts or heals in human relations.

Here is how to have right attitudes towards troublesome people. See them as scared people, for that is what they are. Their unkindness is an inevitable outcome of their anxiety. Their behaviour is compulsive. They cannot recognize self-harming behaviour even when suffering from it.

See them as scared, but add neither sentimentality nor compromise. Sentimentality includes self-pity. Compromise towards others reveals compromise towards oneself. Both attitudes cause wrong behaviour towards troublesome people, later regretted. A clear mind builds quality in human relations.

QUANDARY OF A STUDENT

Charles said, 'Since this is only my third meeting I am in a quandary over many things.'

'What is one of them?'

'At the last meeting you advised us to make connections between various ideas. What does this mean?'

'Take two ideas and connect them until a third factor appears — that of perception. For instance, connect the virtue of self-responsibility with the idea of wild emotions. Try to see the many connections here. For one, a person who permits himself to be carried away by reckless feelings is responsible for where they take him. He has abandoned his right to not be psychologically kidnapped, so envy or worry is his own fault. Perception here builds watchfulness over psychic property. In spare moments during your day, make these connections.'

QUENCH ESCAPISM

A new student asked his teacher, 'How can I make the crooked places straight?'

'Take as a fact what you now take as an insult.'

'Details, please.'

'Most people fail to change themselves because they wrongly take self-facts as insults. A weak man glares angrily when told of his weakness. A woman who cherishes self-pity will resent any probing into her secret love. They take facts as insults instead of as healing medicines. Facing negative features is our only chance for dissolving them. Only a faced negative fact can be changed into a positive fact.'

'But self-confrontation is so painful!'

'The pain itself has a false foundation. You feel pain only when an ideal but false self-image is threatened with exposure by the fact of your actual condition. No false self-picture, no pain. The entire secret of success is to quench escapism.'

QUERY ABOUT ASSISTANCE

The conversation with Mr and Mrs M. began with a discussion of good and evil. Mrs M. remarked, 'We finally saw what you meant when stating that all evil is simply a state of psychic unconsciousness. This means that self-awakening is the only power for true goodness.'

Added Mr M., 'Man is like an incomplete house. You do not see an unfinished house as evil, but you do see it as terribly inconvenient.'

Mrs M. asked, 'Why is it so difficult to find genuine assistance for the inner voyage?'

'Because you cannot gain guidance towards the harbour from a man in the same drifting boat that you occupy. If you want to conquer fear and depression, can a fearful and depressed man help you? But the other man will never admit he is as lost as you are, for he lives by false advantages of pretending to know the way to the harbour. The question is, do you really want the harbour or do you want pleasantly deceptive advice that carries you deeper into the fog? If you want the harbour, trust your own inner compass.'

QUEST FOR SMOOTH SEAS

Two human beings meet for the first time. They may come together for a business transaction, for social affairs, perhaps for romance and marriage. There is one factor which determines the course of the relationship, which makes it smooth or stormy. It is the mental and spiritual level of each person. That is the single determining factor; there is no other.

With this in mind, reflect a moment. Can you imagine how any human being could neglect self-investigation? Is it not incredible that anyone would sail thoughtlessly into a stormy sea?

When finding yourself in a psychic storm, say to yourself, 'There is something in me which encouraged this to happen to the point where it actually happened. I wonder what it was? Impulsiveness? Insecurity? Thoughtlessness? Well, all can be changed. I will transform myself through self-insight, which will change my experiences. This is the main business of my life from now on — the quest for smooth seas.'

QUESTION ABOUT CLASSES

During an informal discussion after class, Keith asked, 'Why is it that one person can get something from esoteric classes, while another cannot?'

'Suppose a man has seriously wondered for years about his life here on earth. While dazed and dissatisfied, he happens to find a book which tells him the truth. It interests him, strikes a responsive chord. Through the book he hears of a class in esotericism. He attends with a friend. The serious man again feels the rightness of what he hears, but the friend feels nothing. Why the difference? The serious man is ready; his friend is not. The friend is still hostile to anything which threatens his pretence of already having his life under control. Make no mistake. A deep part of the friend knows it is hearing the truth, but it feels threatened. Do you know what will happen on the way home? In one way or another the friend will anxiously criticize the lecture. The serious man must refuse to listen to the friend's dishonest attack.'

QUESTION EVERYTHING

During an informal discussion a teacher invited questions from the class. A new student raised his hand to ask, 'May I know my greatest weakness?'

'You never question anything. You are sleepily gullible. Now I will ask you a question. Do you know the foundation of gullibility?'

'No, sir. Please tell me.'

'It is made of many bricks. Mental laziness is one of them. You find it easier to believe what someone says instead of determining its truth or falsity by independent investigation. A needless timidity towards the unknown is another. You fear that a new path may lead you too far away from your comfortable but wrong location. I want you to question everything. Now then, do you fully understand all this?'

'Yes, sir.'

'I told you to question everything!'

QUICKNESS OF MIND

As an enlightening experiment, think of a subject you understand thoroughly. It might be something connected with your business or recreation. Say it is real estate. When someone asks you a question about real estate you answer instantly and accurately. You do not need to ponder. Time and hesitation are not involved. You just know. If everyone else on earth argued against your statement you would calmly and confidently rest in your rightness.

A mind which understands itself thoroughly possesses a similar quickness and certainty, though operating on a much higher level. It is never bogged down in theories or indecisions. Out of its clarity there leaps an instant comprehension of every arising situation. This swiftness has nothing to do with impulsive outbursts so commonly witnessed. The self-commanding mind takes a calm look, comprehends immediately, then acts if necessary with pure action.

QUIET MIND

Ordinary thinking cannot solve personal problems because ordinary thinking is the very cause of problems. A farmer does not ask the wolf for help in protecting the sheep. Every human being who has ever had a problem somehow senses this fact. He knows very well that he never really solves a difficulty; he only shoves it into a cupboard to make room for the next one. Out of his frenzy he reasons, 'If only I could stop thinking about this crisis. If only I could free my mind from its own chaos.'

He is closer than he realizes.

Any man or woman can develop the ability to not think in ordinary ways. This is the same as thinking from a higher level, with a new mind which is not enslaved by mechanicalness.

You can start by sitting quietly by yourself. Do not try to do anything with your mind. Just watch it do whatever it wants to do. Become acquainted with arising and disappearing thoughts. This experiment may feel strange at first, but persist. You will eventually catch your first glimpse of a mind which is not ordinary. It is the quiet mind which has power to solve all problems because it is not a problem to itself.

QUIVERING MAN

One day a quivering man visited a teacher to plead, 'Please help me find myself.'

During the discussion a messenger of the troubled man appeared. 'I thought you would like to know,' said the messenger, 'that your business affairs took a sudden turn towards prosperity.'

The visitor exclaimed to the teacher, 'Ah! I feel better now. Goodbye.'

A month later the still-troubled man returned to repeat his

sorrowful request. 'Please help me. I cannot bear my agony.'

The messenger appeared a second time, saying with a sly grin, 'A beautiful woman awaits you at home.'

The visitor leaped up to gasp, 'All is well! Goodbye!'

A friend of the teacher asked him, 'How often will that quivering man repeat this pattern of behaviour?'

Sighed the teacher, 'Until he sees.'

QUIZZING FOR INSIGHT

A teacher instructed his students, 'For more guiding light, quiz yourself constantly.' He then provided these examples:

'Do I know that frustration can lead to liberation instead of to discouragement?'

'Why do I make shallow assumptions when I can have the powerful facts?'

'If overwhelmed by defeatism, I can recall that Reality does not believe in that state, so why should I?'

'Can I see that being considerate of another person consists largely in not interfering with him?'

'Do I really see the folly of being praised by deluded people?'

'Am I aware that only a different kind of human being can recognize another different man or woman?'

'How deeply do I see through the colourful paint with which people coat themselves to see them as they really are?'

'Have I ever considered how worthwhile it is to learn how to not suffer from myself?'

REACTIONS

Everyone hearing pure truth has a dominating reaction which is opposed by a smaller attitude. He may be:

Puzzled, but interested in hearing more.
Hopeful, but blocked by feelings of guilt.
Hostile, but sensing the rightness of the message.
Attracted, but anxious over leaving habitual ways.
Disdainful, but curious over the freshness of truth.
Receptive, but worried by what others may think.
Attentive, but having little sincerity.
Nervous, but willing to endure more lessons.
Encouraged, but too confused to persist.
Inspired, but doubtful over the next step.

A person's reaction is determined by his level of cosmic maturity. Those ready for higher levels will place their whole being on the side of positive attitudes. Two good attitudes are an interest in hearing more and a willingness to endure the nervousness felt when truth challenges fanciful imagination.

REAL INSPIRATION

A class in Chicago requested, 'Please give us something to think about.'

'Your own nature is the only reward or punishment you receive on earth. What you are is how you feel. There is no division between the kind of person you are and the feelings you have. You yourself are your very feelings. Connect this with another point. When suffering, you suffer only from yourself, regardless of how you think it is caused by external happenings.'

Someone commented, 'We sense the truth of that, but it still makes us uncomfortable.'

'As uncomfortable as it may feel, nothing is more inspiring than a blunt fact about oneself. As pleasant as it may sound, nothing is more discouraging than a falsehood about oneself masquerading as a fact.'

'With all this in mind, when can we expect real inspiration?'

'When there is no difference between the way you appear and the way you are.'

REALNESS

Mr and Mrs R. told the class they had been discussing an interesting topic at home. 'What does it mean to be a real person?' said Mr R. 'That is what we wanted to know.'

'We have picked up good clues here in class,' added Mrs R., 'but could we search it out some more?'

'Being a real person must be studied from a special viewpoint. Have you ever noticed how you are one person in a certain situation and quite another elsewhere? You may behave in a certain manner towards someone you want to impress, but act quite differently with a family member. A man contains dozens of conflicting personalities, each leaping on stage for a moment, only to be replaced by the next clever actor. Realization of his multiple personality is a man's first step towards realness and unification. As self-knowledge banishes this noisy mob, it makes room for the real.'

RECEIVE LIBERTY

Imagine yourself standing outside a fire station when sirens scream and firemen clamber on to their engines. As a fireman dashes by you ask, 'Where are you going?'

Responds the fireman, 'To a fire that happened ten years ago.'

You think you must be dreaming. Something is wrong. Firemen do not race to fires that happened ten years ago.

Yet we behave just as strangely when responding with wild emotions to events of ten or fifty years ago.

We must cut the cord of time which binds us to the past. We must cut ourselves away from unconscious responses arising from past defeats and sorrows.

Right now, receive your liberty.

RECOGNITION OF AUTHENTIC HELP

The only man who really believes in you is the man who believes in himself. His belief is not the lazy and gullible kind arising from self-deception and superstition. It is the kind founded on knowledge acquired through right inner adventuring. The foundation is made of facts, not fantasies. A person living in dreamland cannot possibly believe in your opportunity for self-newness. How can he? Newness does not exist to him.

It does exist to certain rare individuals. Historically, Christ, Buddha and Lao-tse were among those who lived what they taught. Having found the treasure for themselves, they knew it was universal and limitless. That is why they gave freely.

How might you recognize such a rare individual today? How might you recognize a man who really believes in you? A certain amount of personal action is necessary. This action must attract to you a certain amount of the uniqueness possessed fully by the enlightened teacher. Climb a mile or two up the side of a mountain. See that man on top of the mountain? Your own climbing brought him into sight.

REFLECT NEW LIFE

An archaeologist in Egypt once uncovered a statue which had been hidden for centuries in the desert sands. At first glance the statue appeared dull and commonplace. But when placed in a position to receive sunrays, 'It was as if it had come to life.'

No matter how long we have been out of sight of ourselves, we can reflect new life. Feeling lost is nothing more than a gigantic misunderstanding which you can toss out. Feeling dull is simply the result of wrong learning, which you can unlearn.

Most people are motivated by what they want from the world of people and events. Futility wins. Let yourself be motivated by what you want from the invisible world. You win.

REJECT SELF-CONDEMNATION

Self-condemnation and self-dislike are wrong moves. They are two bars in the prison cell. If you did not condemn yourself you would be free of all condemnation, for no other person possesses the right or the power to condemn you. If another person blames you, that is a wrong move on his part. By condemning you he feels self-approval by comparison, which is vanity.

But a refusal of self-blame is no excuse for seeing how much we must do with and for ourselves. A marathon runner does not impose moral judgment upon the defects in his stride, nor does he ignore them. He examines his stride with but one purpose in mind — to run smoother and faster.

When this was discussed in a class in Tennessee, someone asked, 'Please review why self-condemnation is a wrong move.'

'It is wrong because it keeps alive the illusion that one possesses a separate self, a labelled identity. Each time you condemn yourself you reinforce this false belief, which perpetuates the suffering it causes.'

RELAXED POWER

When you are completely powerless — and understand what this means from the esoteric viewpoint — you have an entirely new kind of power. Unlike power and authority on the social level, this power is relaxed, for it has no oppositions and no enemies who must be watched. This is the peaceful power of the single-minded man.

If this esoteric viewpoint is not clear to you, have patience. When watering your garden you may not understand the process by which the underground water works on the roots. However, you can clearly see the results in blooming flowers and tasty fruits. In the same manner, our right internal gardening will produce new life with no concern nor bewilderment on our part.

RELIABLE PRINCIPLES
Cosmic principles are supremely honest and reliable. They deliver an abundance of whatever has been promised. Wish to rise above your present self? You will be shown how. Want to know how to brighten what happens to you? Instructions will be complete. Your part? Just come with something right, perhaps a steadfast wish for help, or even with a weariness with the old ways. The following paragraph shows how it goes.

A man with something right in him reads an esoteric book to gain knowledge. This he wins, but also experiences discomfort. Disturbance is present because his rightness urges him to vigorously toss out those parts which are comfortable and familiar but wrong. He is like a prisoner-of-war who has escaped the enemy camp but has a lingering yearning for its strange security. Though challenged by unfamiliar surroundings, such a psychological prisoner is in an excellent position. A willingness to endure unknown territory gradually turns into a compass. Additional reading will show him how to avoid enemy soldiers and reach the border of a friendly nation.

RELIEVING INSIGHT
From the viewpoint of Reality there are no answers to questions such as 'Should I get married?' and 'How can I become an important person?' The awakened man sees the very questions as false, for they are taken from the immense bag of illusions carried by mankind. Both questions wrongly assume that a change in exterior conditions can bring happiness to the inner person. Both sacrifice contentment in the here and now to some supposed satisfaction in the vague and distant future.

If people could only see that the true answer to such questions resides in the very disappearance of the question!

Great relief accompanies this insight.

REMEMBER
Our problem is forgetfulness — forgetfulness of who we really are, of where we can go, of how we can change, of what we can attain.

The solution is to remember. Remember what?

That whatever is truly valuable can never be threatened or destroyed by exterior events.

That the kind of nature you have is the only reward and the only punishment you have.

That freedom does not consist of behaving as we wish, but in behaviour which includes no self-harming wishes.

That no one needs to fight to keep his world together, for that is simply achieved by being one with the world.

That the only motive you need for walking the esoteric path is because it is the right thing to do — right for you.

REMEMBERED WORDS
A remembered word can serve as a psychological sheepdog to prevent us from wandering on to rocky ground. Let each of these words turn you back towards green meadows:

Examine
Simplify
Try
Relax
Aim
Ponder
Practice
Advance

Take the word *ponder*. Ponder this fact: There is an inward place having nothing to do with unhappiness. You can learn to live from this peaceful place. Ponder that fact until living it.

RESCUE FROM BLUNDERS
We will never understand why human events happen as they do by looking into history or science. We can understand

them only by looking into human nature. How easily we overlook the plain fact that events unfold according to human desires and motives. But, of course, self-investigation is the last thing that ego-defending men want to go into. You cannot get through to self-deceived man because one of his strongest illusions is that he is not self-deceived. Remember, fact can be separated from fantasy only by the person who chooses fact over fantasy.

Facts can save anyone from anything. And you can get the facts just as fast as you want them. Maybe you worry about making blunders, as did one inquirer. What helpful facts were needed by this worrier? He was told, 'You must have no fear of blunders, but must study them with a scientific state of mind. And remember, a scientific study of mistakes does not include self-defence. You cannot even correct a mistake in spelling if you defend your error. Be teachable about blunders. That ends them.'

RESISTANCE

'You have made me aware of my resistance to the rescuing facts,' said Paul. 'I see how I used to refuse to listen to anything outside of my cramped mind. As you described it, I was living in the closet of a sixty-room mansion. May we have some comments on the problem of resistance?'

'How on earth can we learn by being told things we think we already understand? We learn only by being told what we don't comprehend. That is plain logic, but how many people are logical? Very few. Fear of the unknown. There is the barrier. But since the known has delivered nothing but grief, the solution must be in exploring the unknown. More logic. Dare to see what you fear to see. Every liberated person has done this.'

'But I don't know what to do next.'

'Don't resist that state.'

RESPONSIBILITY

Be fully responsible for what happens to you and your life will flow in a new and attractive direction.

Know that self-responsibility is not a burden, as shallow thinkers imagine, but an opportunity for freedom.

Responsibility does not exist in the man who must be surrounded by those who agree with his opinions.

Take personal responsibility for the way you feel and you will soon begin to feel different.

Authentic responsibility develops according to the number of esoteric tasks we set for ourselves.

Abandonment of individual responsibility has a treacherous pleasure which deceives and punishes millions of people.

Awareness of lack of responsibility may be surprising at first, but it opens the door to lasting treasures.

Make yourself responsible for the way you are treated by other people and there will be a change in treatment.

The truly responsible man or woman is one who seeks and finds the cosmic kingdom within.

RETURN TO FUNDAMENTALS

Whenever you do not know what to do about a bothersome condition, return to the fundamentals. Somewhere among them you will find the right key. Perhaps you need reminding that the battle is not against people and events, but against personal psychic hypnosis. Maybe you need to remember that it is good, not bad, to see how little you know, for that invites rescuing knowledge.

There is special value in returning for a second look at a principle we think we already understand. This is what Martha did, with good results. She told the class, 'I believed I knew the cause and cure for mental pains, but a recent experience told me otherwise. So I will return to a basic question. How can I escape mental anguish?'

'Mental anguish always connects in some way with lack of Oneness. To say it differently, anguish occurs because we falsely think we have an ego which is apart from events, and so we also falsely think we must fight events which seem to oppose the ego. When there is no false self to fight an event, anguish cannot exist.'

REVIEW THE FACTS

'I am like someone who has been reading a mystery novel for several months but can't get to the last chapter. I mean I can't solve the mystery of why so many unpleasant things happen to me. I am seeking a solution to my confusion.'

'Confusion may be a fact of your experience but it is not a necessity of your life. Review the fundamental facts you have absorbed, for example, remember to let events fall on your willingness to understand, not on your resistance to truth. Also remember that solutions come to a quiet mind. Learn your psychic lessons one step at a time.'

'How can I repel hostile attitudes from others?'

'The need to repel means they have reached and hurt you. When you no longer have anything in you which corresponds with their hostility you are unreachable. You can learn a great secret. It is the secret of disappearing psychologically. In other words, there is no one there to get hurt.'

RIGHT ATTITUDES

Several new students attended their first class in esoteric wisdom. Their teacher told them, 'Please remember the importance of having right attitudes towards the lessons you are about to receive.' Nodding to a group of advanced students, the teacher requested, 'Please supply some of these right attitudes.'

One man responded, 'Give the truth a warm welcome, remembering that its only aim is to cure whatever is wrong.'

A woman stated, 'Never reject an idea just because it is new and unfamiliar to you.'

A third student added, 'Realize that authentic self-change can occur only with a courageous willingness to change.'

RIGHT EFFORT

Richard raised his hand to admit, 'I am confused about effort. At one time we are told to make enthusiastic effort towards self-change, but at other times we are instructed to live casually and effortlessly.'

'It depends upon your motive. What do you want from

your effort? You can make effort to prove yourself right or you can make effort to be right. The kind of world you inhabit depends upon your choice.'

'What,' asked Carol, 'is an example of false proving?'

'In an attempt to prove the possession of a dynamic personality, some people use the smallest incident as an excuse for an emotional outburst. They have wrong motives, make wrong efforts, get wrong results.'

Richard resumed, 'How can we stay on course?'

'Maintain right effort by serving your real nature, not that nervous impostor who runs around in your name.'

RIGHT LOYALTY

A battle in a war was described as 'a battle of wretched blunders'. Both sides in the battle committed foolish and costly mistakes.

Likewise, wretched and blundering man battles through his days, never questioning whether the battle need be fought at all.

Have you ever calmly questioned your ways? If not, the very questioning can be the start of a new way. Do not think you are being disloyal to anyone or anything by asking questions about your life here on earth. You owe no loyalty to sources of disorder. Do not listen to anyone who tries to chain you to confusion. Listen to your own original mind. Be loyal to your real nature. That is the same as being loyal to God, to Reality.

RIGHT MOTIVES

There was once a vast desert where water was scarce. However, one energetic traveller discovered a new oasis having an abundance of pure water. He remained there as keeper of the oasis.

Having a penetrating mind, the keeper saw instantly the motives of travellers who requested water. The deceit and hypocrisy of human beings was clear to him. One man said he wished water for his family, but the keeper knew he wanted to sell it at a profit. Another traveller pleaded for water for his horses, but the keeper knew he would keep it all for himself. The keeper reflected, 'They have their own impure water for travelling the desert, and hope that trickery will obtain the pure.'

So only the travellers with right motives received pure water.

You, the reader, know the lesson.

RIGHTNESS AND PEACE

'At any precise moment,' stated Wesley, 'I have a dozen small wars raging inside me. The fury may not show on my face because I am an experienced actor on the social stage. My question is, how can I end the battle?'

'Please listen carefully to this answer. Do not take it as a moral teaching or as religious sentiment. Take it as solid fact. Will you do that?'

Wesley nodded.

'Rightness is total power. Nothing can harm the person living in rightness. I am not talking about human viewpoints towards rightness; I am talking about rightness itself. Have Cosmic Rightness and the battle ends.'

RIGHT ORDER

Set your life in its right order. Lay a solid foundation and build upward. Here are several right orders to live by:

Co-operate first with your own nature, for that creates uncompromising co-operation with other people.

Ask spiritual questions with intense integrity, and inspiring answers will surely arrive.

Teach yourself, after which you can teach those who want to know what you have learned.

Understand the kind of mind you operate from, which will show you why you do what you do.

Wish to learn all about your viewpoints, instead of wishing to defend your present viewpoints.

Be conscious of what you are about to say, then speak, for that will produce correct speech.

Live rightly with yourself, after which you will live rightly with every circumstance that comes along.

ROLES AND REALITIES

'Most of us play roles of one kind or another,' stated Bert. 'Please discuss the harm it does.'

'One way to block happiness is to pretend to already be happy. The role-player becomes the prisoner of his role. It will always be unconscious play-acting, so we must first suspect that it is a role and not a reality. An earnest person can easily do this. He can honestly ask whether he is really happy, or merely playing the public role of a happy person. It is not difficult to see through the play-acting of others. You don't need complicated psychological tests to determine what a man is really like. Just watch his face when he is either flattered or insulted. You will see a slave to external influences, which is one unhappy result of role-playing.'

S

SECRET CODE

A secret agent was sent to a warlike country to collect information. His task was to determine the strength and the intentions of the enemy country. A simple but effective method was used to send information back to his superior officers. In seemingly innocent letters to his own country he casually included pairs of numbers, such as five and twelve, and thirty-six and eight. The received letters were quickly decoded.

How? The secret agent possessed a copy of a book which had sold millions of copies around the world. He used it to send his messages back home. For example, the numbers five and twelve indicated *page five, twelfth word*; while thirty-six and eight meant page *thirty-six, eighth word*. Anyone knowing the secret code could read the messages.

Esoteric information is available to all. However, individual effort must be made to learn its secret code. Fortunately, the code is located where every man can find it — within his own nature.

SECRET MOTIVES

Remarked Marie in class, 'I find it difficult to understand human nature and human relations. Sometimes I get hurt.'

'Think of something you do understand and understand clearly. Take the time you try to tell your child something for his own benefit, such as advising him to study his school lessons. You can see by his face that he does not hear you at all; his mind is three blocks away, climbing a tree. This clearness will expand to other areas as you continue to work internally. Among other rewards, you will see straight into the secret motives of scheming people, which protects you from them.'

'It is curious that you brought that up,' said Marie. 'More and more I realize the need to see people as they are, not as gullibility makes them appear to be.'

SEE SOMETHING

Be true to yourself, not to ideas you have about yourself. Have you ever noticed the number of self-descriptions maintained within? Take a quiet and thoughtful look.

See the difference between your natural self and your described self. The presence of a described self is easily detected. Any feelings of worry or pressure, any painful compulsion to prove oneself, indicates that a memorized version of oneself is operating destructively.

You need not memorize who you are. That is futile and exhausting. It is like an effort to keep clothes on a scarecrow in a strong wind. It keeps you running frantically into the field to keep things looking right.

Forget who you are. Forget who you assume you must become. You do not have to become someone. You already are. But that someone has no description and needs none.

Forget what you *call* yourself. Try it. See what happens. Nothing harmful can happen. You will see something. But you must do it.

SELF-CONTRADICTIONS

Fred always came early and occupied a front seat. One night he commented, 'We are so unaware of the ways we injure ourselves. Could you please make one of them clear to us?'

'See self-contradictions. Be aware of how one part of you is opposed by another part. This means you are at war with yourself. Guess who gets wounded?'

'I know we must think for ourselves,' Fred went on, 'but I'll ask anyway. What is an example of self-contradiction, and how can we work on it?'

'The next time you state your motive for doing something, remember the motive you gave. Then, look deeply into yourself until seeing the real motive.'

The class laughed. Fred nodded and remarked, 'All this seems terribly important to understand.'

'You have no idea how important.'

SELF-IMAGES

In a group meeting in Ohio the topic turned to self-images. Morton commented, 'From what you have said in past lectures we must put an end to all kinds of self-images. This includes, you said, both images of weakness and those in which we see ourselves as strong and confident. Why must self-images go?'

'Because an image is nothing but an image. You are no more your images than you are a photograph of yourself. Any attempt to prove an image, such as a self-picture of being authoritative, only sinks you deeper into the marsh of confusion and despair. You also deny yourself entrance into the authentic strength of Reality. Nothingness has nothing to contribute. Suppose someone told you to get a drink of water from a desert mirage. You would wonder what was wrong with him. Understand?'

'Suppose we drop our self-imaginations. What takes their place?'

'Why don't you find out?'

SELF-NEWNESS

A clear and beautiful stream ran through the centre of a small village. It gave great pleasure to the citizens to just sit quietly and watch its casual flow. But through carelessness, junk was allowed to fall into the stream, spoiling its purity. The aroused citizens took action. When foreign objects were banned from the stream, it returned to its original purity.

We purify ourselves by not renewing our negative nature each day. Read that sentence again: *We purify ourselves by not renewing our negative nature each day.* That is enough. That is right action. Self-newness appears by itself as we cease to toss foreign objects into the mental stream. One person must end bitterness, while another must no longer feel cheated. But all can return to the original purity of his flowing mind.

SELF-NOTICING

Just as the wings of birds have no meaning to a rabbit, unseen facts have no reality to a man. So the great question is, how do you get him to see what he cannot see?

Teach him the art of self-noticing.

Impress upon yourself the necessity and the wisdom of constant self-noticing. This watchfulness is not the same as worriedly thinking about yourself. Esoteric self-noticing consists of standing aside as a passive observer of whatever you do and feel. Just alertly notice whatever is there. For instance, you might notice the failure of your efforts to find real and lasting satisfaction. Or you notice how a thrill is always followed by a depression. That is excellent self-action. It loosens the chains which bind an individual to dissatisfaction and depression. Facts are attracting freedom.

SELF-SPONTANEITY

A boy was standing with his father on the bank of a sparkling stream. Being too young to understand natural power, the boy asked, 'What keeps the river flowing past us?'

Answered the father, 'It comes from a higher place than here.'

Remember, the real solution to any problem resides in a higher place than the problem. The mental level which creates a difficulty cannot cure it. We must look higher than our present level.

To discover self-spontaneity is one of the great discoveries of life. Spontaneity frees us of so much which is burdensome and compulsive in society. By first wishing to become a true person within, we put an end to the compulsive tasks which make days so dreadful to most people. Free from a false sense of social duties, we are also free of its accompanying tensions and false guilts. In this newness we are true contributors to society, first by not adding to the confusion, and next by giving truth to those who want it. Discover self-spontaneity.

SELF-VICTORY

It is possible for anyone to command his own mind. We do not permit strangers to enter our home and destroy valuable possessions, so why permit negative thoughts to roam destructively around our minds? You are no more required to submit to treacherous thoughts than you are required to submit to deceitful people — but you must learn to recognize treachery when it masquerades as sincerity. You can find all the weapons necessary for commanding your own mind, such as right intentions and a wish to end mental storms.

Conquer yourself, for then all haunting questions regarding the conquest of life will be answered. Then, never again will you need to anxiously pursue anything at all. Self-victory is total victory.

SHOCKING EXPERIENCES

Before asking questions, Douglas spoke of his efforts to make a new life for himself. Everything had failed, he said, leaving him discouraged and bewildered. 'As my first question,' he said, 'I would like to know how to respond rightly to a shocking experience.'

'Refuse to be hypnotized by it. Have you ever noticed how a shocking experience hypnotizes the mind by unreeling maddening mental movies? Work against this. Do so by standing aside and observing the mental movies instead of letting them take you over. There is a part of you which is quite capable of standing apart to calmly study the experience. It is like sitting in your home and watching a violent movie on television. You see what is going on, but do not refer the violence back to yourself. Practise this with both small and large experiences. Someday you will see yourself as apart from both interior and exterior shocks.'

SILENT STATEMENT

At a certain place along the path you may have to make a silent statement to relatives and friends. You might declare, 'It is possible that my change of attitudes and actions displease you. I do not want to hurt you in any way, but I must begin to live my own life. I can no longer go along with the old and self-punishing ways. If you wish to go with me, we can work together to find the way out. If you do not, then I must go alone. We may continue with our usual relationship in everyday affairs, but inwardly I must take another path. I am not sure where I am going, but I know it is the right and necessary course to take.'

This must not be said in self-dramatics, but because the wish to find the exit to the cave has become the dominating force in one's life.

SIMPLE REMEDY

One cause of anxiety is an attempt to be what you think the other person wants you to be. This causes painful self-splitting. One part of you tries to live up to the other person's expectations, while another part wants to relax and be natural. This anxiety has another anxiety behind it. We try to please other people so that they will not leave us, so that they will remain as companion or friend or sex partner.

The simple remedy is to be yourself. There is never a need to ever be what the other person desires you to be. Pass from slavery to freedom by being what you really want to be. You really want to be yourself. In that natural state there is no anxiety over losing anyone or anything.

SLEEPING POWERS

'What power does a truly awakened man possess that enables him to help troubled humanity?'

'He sees human beings in an entirely different way than they see themselves.'

'For example?'

'He sees how they label weaknesses as strengths. People are proud of their bad tempers. They feel elated when getting revenge on someone. But an awakened man also knows about sleeping powers in human beings. If they would listen, he could show them how to chase the haunting ghosts out of their minds.'

'So the task of an awakened man is to help us remember and revive the powers of our real nature.'

'Yes. When a man starts on the path, he is like someone trying to remember the words of a favourite song he knew many years ago.'

SPEAK FROM YOURSELF
Speaking from ourselves means to speak from a nature not influenced by past conditioning. Therefore, whoever speaks from himself is someone who has explored and travelled beyond the jungle of society's negative conditioning. Most people are firmly convinced they possess individual expression, but their words and ideas are unconsciously borrowed from the past. Few ever realize this, for a tape-recorder does not know it is a tape-recorder.

A man wishing to make a good impression on others does not speak from himself. He speaks from an acquired need to be accepted or to gain imagined advantages. A person speaking from anxiety does not express his original nature, but merely turns loose a mechanical habit picked up from other anxious people, perhaps his parents. A liberated nature has no such anxiety.

Suppose you were in a room containing five men who really spoke from themselves. While using their individual modes of expression, all would say the same thing about Reality. Why? Because the truth is not contradictory, as are man-made words. Reality is One.

SPECIAL METHOD
One week a teacher employed a special method for teaching his disciples the lessons they needed. Everyone who complained of injustice or persecution was told, 'Find your illusion.'

'I give much but get little,' sighed one student.

'Find your illusion.'

'Everything is against me,' said another pupil.

'Find your illusion.'

That special method can serve us also.

It is an illusion that self-satisfaction can be gained by going out and meeting other people. A man may go out with the aim of gaining money or excitement or sex or allies. Even when getting what he wants he always makes the same blunder. He never sees that he remains exactly the same person he was before — the same nervous and irritable slave to compulsive cravings. He must see that only a change of nature — a real change — can alter the way he acts and feels and responds.

STONE STATUE

During one class session the tragic human condition came up for discussion. 'The liberating truth is certainly available,' said a student to the teacher, 'but when will men receive it?'

The teacher replied, 'In the city park there is a stone statue of a famous military hero. When it responds to the truth, so will the masses of men respond. See the similarities in man's condition and the statue? Both are hardened. Both maintain a fixed position, unable to see anything outside their narrow view. Neither possesses cosmic hearing. For something good to happen, the stone statue must be removed and replaced with a real human being. A real man is not fixed; he can go places.'

STRANGE FACT

'You have said we do not think deeply enough to see the startling significance of certain ideas. Please give us one such idea.'

'Whoever blames another person for his troubles is making a terrible confession. He admits he does not think for himself. Think deeply about that.'

'Our quest for happiness runs into so many puzzling choices!'

'Make up your mind to command yourself and you will

never have to make up your mind regarding happiness. A free mind rests in contentment above baffling choices.'

'When walking along the esoteric path I sometimes feel that I don't know where I am going.'

'Congratulations! You must *not* know where you are going. If you can describe the distant scenery, how can it be the new and different land you seek? As strange as it sounds, the more you walk in darkness the faster you walk towards sunlight.'

STRENGTHENING PRINCIPLES

When refusing to run away from unhappy feelings, you force them, by psychological law, to run away from you.

There are possibilities for the person who can state an opinion and not think the statement creates the fact.

The right reaction to the unknown is to experience it, not fear it.

By enduring rejection to the very end, the very idea of rejection disappears from both your vocabulary and your day.

The difference between living from the part of your mind called memory and living from the whole mind is the difference between night and day.

It is only by doing something truly different that we attain something truly different.

Avoid complacency by returning regularly to basic truths with a wish to see their deeper meanings.

STRENGTH THROUGH UNDERSTANDING

Eugene, a member of a class in Texas, stood up one evening. 'I would like to tell about an inspiring experience I had recently,' he said. 'It may help others. When first coming to the group I sensed that the teacher saw through me. Since no man wants his follies out in the open, it made me nervous. This went on until an encouraging thought struck me. I realized that his very power of insight was power for authentic assistance. Only a person who understands another can help him.'

Eugene concluded, 'It is astonishing how beginners refuse the very food that could end their hunger. What I first feared became my source of real confidence.'

STOP FIGHTING

Troubled human beings have everything exactly backward. They think that by winning they can stop fighting. The opposite is true. By ceasing to fight, you win — but what you win is superior and different from what was imagined. A man believes he can end the terrible inner battle by winning wealth or power or endless sexual experiences. If winning them he is dismayed to find that the battle is not over; he must continue the weary fight. His despair is overwhelming, for his dream has turned into a nightmare of compulsive craving.

Stop fighting and you win. Stop fighting and you end the illusion that you must win. You have already won, but you do not understand what this means. Find out.

STRONG MEDICINE

Over the years a certain teacher had studied the thousands of people who had attended his classes for the first time. Having the X-ray mind of an awakened man, he saw through human nature. He was not deceived by the impulsive enthusiasms displayed by people after hearing the first lecture. He knew that most of them would fall away after falling once more under the hypnotic influence of their own conditioned minds.

Consequently, under certain conditions, his first talk to new people consisted only of these words: 'Today, I wish you to understand just one thing. In tomorrow's lecture, you will be told many things you will not want to hear. Your habitual nature will rebel against and even silently attack many ideas given you. But to be helped, you must be given strong medicine. So keep that in mind, then know you are welcome to come again tomorrow if you wish.'

STUBBORN MAN

A stubborn man told a friend, 'No one is going to tell me what to do. I want my own way.'

'There is something you should hear,' began the friend, but the stubborn man did not hear it. He had already rushed into the world to get his own way.

A few weeks later the bruised and depressed stubborn man staggered back to his friend. He complained, 'I have had nothing but fights and defeats. Why didn't you tell me it would be like this?'

Asked the friend, 'Would you have listened?'

Ignoring the question, the stubborn man slid his chair closer and confided, 'Here is what I want. I want my own way but do not want to pay the consequences for it. You are my friend. Show me how.'

'What you ask is impossible. Definite cosmic laws cover this. The man who tosses a handful of dust will get it back in his own face.'

Rising, the stubborn man spoke sarcastically. 'I ask for advice and you give me philosophy. Goodbye. I will find someone who really knows the answer.'

SUBMISSION IS UNNECESSARY

The trouble is, a man submits. Unconscious submission is his way of life. He bows sullenly before circumstances instead of conquering them by understanding his right relationship to them. He is not opposed by any circumstance because he does not exist as an individual ego, therefore, there can be nothing opposed to that false self. Where there is no one to fight an enemy, there can be no enemy.

Remember, to not submit does not mean to worriedly fight a circumstance. The very fighting is what gives the condition the illusion of having power over you. Fighting keeps the illusion alive, just as bouncing a ball seems to give the ball power of its own. No bouncer, no bouncing. The correct alternative to submission is to see life as it is, not as it appears to be.

Study this section with care, then submit no longer. See

submission as completely unnecessary.

SUCCESSES

'I want to succeed inwardly but don't know how.'

'Certain facts are possessed by everyone, including you. Stick with those facts. Think about them at every opportunity. Even a bit of understanding is a cosmic magnet which attracts more understanding.'

'I do have one fact about my present ways. I see how wrong and useless they are.'

'That is a marvellous fact. Be glad you have it. It is one kind of success. Try to realize it even more deeply. Do not spare yourself.'

'What other kind of successes will be attracted?'

'Just as certain as sunrise you will some day feel the difference between an excitement aroused by an exterior event and the unique thrill of truth-sensing. This indicates you are no longer depending upon favourable exterior events to provide a feeling of self-importance. In turn, this indicates you are no longer a slave to exterior happenings. Success in the invisible world has placed the visible world under your command.'

SUNSHINE AND SHADOW

A student of esoteric wisdom was seated outdoors, reading an interesting and informative book. He looked up to see that the shadow of a tall tree was advancing towards him. He returned to his reading until noticing that the shadow had reached his foot. He glanced up once more when the shadow had reached his waist. He then became clearly aware of the shadow as it covered the page he was reading. Wishing for more light on the page, he moved his chair, placing himself completely in sunshine once more.

As he sat there he reflected, 'That is just what this book teaches. While there are shadows in the world, they need not cover me. I can change my position and remain in sunlight. All it takes is wise action. I will search out the nature of this wise action.'

SUPREME LIFE

Quite definitely, Supreme Life exists within everyone. It can be called God, the Inner Kingdom, Cosmic Energy or anything else, for words are not important. What is important is to not try to imagine the nature of this superior force. Imagination is a wall preventing direct contact with this natural possession. Imagination is but one small part of our psychic system, so it must not be permitted to speak for the whole person. Also, imagination can only repeat the same old things, for it gets its information from memory, and memory is fixed in the past. Anyone living in the past can never know the freshness of the here and now.

So detect how imagination tries to dominate the mind, how it brazenly pretends to know what it does not really know. Then refuse to let it repeat the same old tiring preachings, do not let it speak for the whole person. Daily practice here breaks down the wall between the individual and Supreme Life. The person then *is* Supreme Life.

SURPRISING DISCOVERY

Asked Arnold, 'How can we tell whether a teaching offered to us rings true or not?'

'There is only one way. There must be at least a small part within you that rings true. This part knows instantly whether a teaching is true or false. Awaken this total intelligence. Some day you may be surprised to discover that one small part of you was right after all.'

'How can we awaken this new intelligence?'

'Do not live like most people. Most human beings want to blame others for their troubles. Assume complete responsibility for what happens to you until you understand the law of cause and effect. An awakened person never causes trouble for himself.'

SWITCH TO SELF-INSIGHT

Imagine yourself seated in a cold and uncomfortable room. Wanting to warm yourself, you absently reach for an electric switch and turn it on. But now you feel colder than before, for you accidentally turned on the switch to the fan instead of the heater. Correcting your mistake, you are soon warm and comfortable.

Your shocks in human encounters are similar to electric shocks of current. Switch them on rightly and you feel right; turn the wrong switch and you feel uncomfortable. Remember that a basic rule of esotericism is that all events, including human events, can be switched to self-gain. This self-gain consists of fresh insight which shows you a superior way.

TAKE IT PERSONALLY

A salesman was walking through a busy public park on his way to a customer. He heard someone shout, but was too absorbed in financial figures to pay much attention. All of a sudden his feet went up and the rest of him went down. He found himself sprawled out in a newly-dug ditch. Unhurt but embarrassed, he looked up to see the foreman of a construction company. 'I tried to warn you,' said the foreman, 'but you were miles away.'

The salesman stood up with a grin and a nod. 'I didn't realize you were talking to me. I should have taken it personally.'

Take esoteric messages personally. They are for you, for you as an individual human being.

The human mind operates strangely. A man insists upon personal attention, personal guidance, personal enrichment — but rarely takes the helpful messages personally! The man who falls into psychic ditches is the man who must heed the friendly voice, and so avoid future falls.

TASTE THE TRUTH

A teacher was seated outdoors with his disciples. He wished them to see the need for personal experience with the truth. Holding up a freshly-baked cake, he asked a disciple, 'What does this cake taste like?'

'I do not know, sir. I have not tasted it.'

Said the teacher to a second disciple, 'Taste this cake and describe its taste to us.' When this was done, the teacher spoke again to the first disciple, 'Can you now describe the cake to us?'

'No, sir.'

'Why not?'

'Because a description of the taste is not the taste itself.'

'Very good. You may now taste the cake for yourself.'

TEACHING OTHER PEOPLE

Robert stood up in a class in Florida. He said, 'One of the first rules of esotericism is to speak about these ideas only to those who show genuine interest. Suppose we meet a sincere individual. How might we best help him?'

'By remembering your own early encounters with esoteric truths. Remember how timid and uncertain you were? Remember your resistance to these facts — how you felt threatened by them? Well, put yourself in the other person's place. He feels the same way. He is still in the stage where he feels truth is trying to take something valuable from him. What truth really wants to take is his misery.'

Robert replied with a nod, 'That is exactly right. I was worried and suspicious over what might happen to me. I was about as receptive as a tree. A certain comment of yours helped me. You said that the man who takes it is the man who makes it.'

TEACHINGS

A true teaching emphasizes self-reliance and self-responsibility. This is because it has confidence in the individual. It knows what a man can do for himself. A false teaching may publicly praise these virtues, but secretly scorns them. It knows nothing of the inspiring results of self-help because it has never tried it.

Never accept a teaching which promises a future reward. It will never come. You cannot live on vague promises. Rightness and goodness are now or never. Heaven is not a geographical location, therefore it cannot be reached by travelling in time. Heaven is a state of timeless being. Accept a teaching which encourages, 'Explore the mystery of time until you see yourself as a liberated human being at this very moment. That is the fact of your existence. Stand upon it right now. Continue to stand in spite of all appearances to the contrary. Truth itself will help you do this, and since truth is inward, you can be totally self-reliant and self-responsible.'

TECHNIQUE FOR FREEDOM

Here is a good technique for daily use. Whenever meeting a new idea, ask yourself, 'What. does this mean?' Ask that direct question and then seek the answer. Search with a combination of your own intelligence and esoteric guidance. That is a winning combination.

Suppose you read, 'The only freedom needed is freedom from yourself.' Diligently inquire, 'What does this mean?' Now relax. Do not be afraid to relax completely in the face of this tremendous truth. But let it be a dynamic kind of quietness in which you listen alertly to your original nature which can explain everything perfectly. This kind of quiet alertness can be practised in the middle of a noisy business office or at home. It allows answers to emerge, like a prisoner-of-war escaping the enemy camp.

Ask, 'What does this mean?' Then you will know from yourself that the only freedom needed is freedom from yourself.

THAWING

There are certain words which excellently describe the psychological process we must experience. The word *thawing* is one of them.

Like ice, man is cold and hardened. Even while suffering terribly from his condition he refuses reality's invitation to come out into the psychological sunshine which could thaw him out. All attempts of truth to melt down his assorted fantasies about himself and his role on earth are stubbornly resisted.

His difficulty is an incorrect assumption about his nature. Fearful of vanishing in the sunlight, he crouches in dark despair in his psychological cave. But will he disappear? He has not heard the good news. There is no one there to disappear. There was no one there in the first place; there were only self-labels of an incredible variety. So he has nothing to lose but his hardened labels. Even a small realization of this good news arouses courage for hiking out of the cave. When thawing in sunshine he will smile at his former fears of being a nobody. He has not disappeared. Like ice melting into water, he has become someone different.

THIRD WAY OF THINKING

'I don't know where I should stand in life,' an inquirer told a teacher. 'Should I stand on this side or that side of a political question? Should I stand here or over there when it comes to standards of morality? I am uncertain and nervous.'

'You are anxious because you still think that one side of a social question is right and the other side wrong. Both sides are wrong. Division is wrongness. Never forget that. At present you view social questions from a mind which wants to feel secure by joining a group of believers or its opposite group. It is this craving for so-called psychological security which forces you to take a side. But have you noticed that insecurity continues? Ever notice how scared and nervous your allies are? That is because society is always wrong.'

Concluded the teacher, 'This is unclear to you because you have not as yet entered the third way of thinking, which is above society's sides. Only in this third way of thinking is there true conscience and decency.'

THOUGHTS ABOUT THINKING

'I don't know how to handle tough daily challenges from the exterior world.'

'Let exterior impressions pass through the purification of a clear mind, just as a filter purifies water.'

'My mind seems so limited.'

'You are limited only by unawareness of how you have limited yourself.'

'My thinking needs guidance in distinguishing between

right and wrong.'

'Do not mistake attractiveness for rightness.'

'It is difficult to understand what life is all about.'

'Understanding comes by exploring and explaining yourself to yourself.'

'My faltering mind needs constant encouragement.'

'The absolute fascination of uncovering the mysteries of your mind is a mountain of encouragement.'

'I think it time I made an earnest effort to find myself.'

'Now you are thinking!'

THREE STEPS

We can think rightly or we can think wrongly towards a difficult situation. Here are three right steps to give yourself:

'The difficulty exists because there is something I do not understand about myself and about life in general.'

'With self-investigation it is possible for me to gain this needed understanding.'

'When I finally see things as they are in reality, the difficulty will cease to exist.'

Do not wander away from this simple plan. Apply it day and night. Perhaps you have a strained human relationship. Recall how minds operate on the level of illusion. They crash like recklessly driven cars. But on the cosmic level they blend, like clouds entering each other. Do not try to change the other person. All you need to dissolve the difficulty is to have a cosmic mind of your own, for it knows no problems at all.

TOPICS FOR DAILY ACTION

Give one of the following topics your creative attention for a full day:

The richness of inner maturity.

The wisdom of using energies constructively.

The folly of self-deception.

The desirability of reaching the other shore.

The need of attaining newness of mind.

The attractiveness of whatever is honest.

The courage of refusing society's propaganda.
The genuine pleasure of inner exploration.
The power of trueness to one's original nature.
The refreshment of living simply and naturally.

TOTAL POWER

The only freedom needed is freedom from a wrongly operating mind. But it must be glimpsed that this is the only liberty needed, for that starts the liberating process.

People want to know, 'Suppose I do study and apply these teachings to my inner life. Will it change how I act and also affect what happens to me in daily actions?' The answer is, of course it will influence daily ways, all for the good. When a clay bowl is dipped into silver colouring, both its inside and outside become silver.

When attributing power to truth, never make exceptions, not a single one. Many people do this without realizing it. God, Truth, Reality, each has total power. Alcoholism, problems related to sex, family difficulties, unwanted habits — all fall away from the individual who abandons his old and conditioned nature to live within the new. Truth is like the sky. People may seldom look up, but the sky still covers everything.

TOTAL SUCCESS

'In last week's lecture,' said Edwin, 'you mentioned something that has haunted my mind ever since. You said that people rarely see their need to succeed as human beings. Will you please expand that idea?'

'It is difficult for a man to see that he can succeed as a businessman or husband or friend and still fail as a whole human being. His mind excludes whatever he does not want to see in favour of the pleasing. It is like picking one sweet grape out of a sour bunch and claiming that the whole cluster is sweet. To succeed as a whole human being means to clear heart and mind of all unconscious negativities.'

'And this success is the same as authentic happiness?'

'Succeed in becoming a whole human being. No other

success is necessary for lasting happiness.'

TRAVEL BEYOND

'Why do we fail to enjoy life?'

'Life can be enjoyed only when you do not try to possess it, like a rainbow. Possessiveness is an attempt to build security, but the exact opposite results. Travel beyond the urge to cling to people and objects and see what is on the other side.'

'Recently a group of people tried to force their beliefs on to me. This reckless zeal is characteristic of pressure-groups. What is behind it?'

'Insecure people always try to convert and involve others. It is their desperate and futile attempt to convince themselves of the rightness of their beliefs. The man who really knows where he stands is able to stand alone.'

'What do we need?'

'You need what is essential. If not having it, do not try to cover up the emptiness by calling the non-essential the essential. An empty jar labelled *peaches* is still an empty jar. Call it an empty jar and go out for peaches.'

TROUBLED THOUGHTS

It is not necessary for anyone to remain with troubled thoughts. They can be pushed away the moment they try to invade. This comes by understanding the mind. It is first needful to be aware that we *are* under the tyranny of undesirable thoughts, which is accomplished through alert watchfulness of the mind. Just notice the mental state you are in. We can next realize the strangely hypnotic fascination of negative thoughts, then refuse the punishing fascination. We can then deliberately interrupt the flow of mechanical and unwanted thoughts, to let them be replaced by consciousness of where we are. Just notice where you are and be aware of what you are doing.

Whenever you feel unhappy about anything at all, remember and practise these techniques. You will see unhappiness fade away.

TRUE AND FALSE

A young artist visited the home of an older man who had been an art expert for many years. When falling into a discussion about forged paintings, the expert invited, 'Come into the next room. You can test yourself.'

In the next room the expert explained, 'Here you see a dozen pictures. Some are authentic works of great artists, while others are forgeries. See whether you can tell the difference.'

In spite of a careful study of the paintings, the young artist mistakenly pronounced several of the forgeries as genuine.

'There is a way to tell the difference,' declared the expert, 'such as knowing the ways of a true artist so well that you could never mistake them. Listen carefully and I will show you how to distinguish the true from the false.'

We must be willing to learn the difference between self-healing and self-harming ideas. Then, our own true nature will reveal the difference.

TRUE AND FALSE SECURITY

There is authentic security and there is illusory security. The false is easily seen because it can be felt as nervousness and apprehension. If we feel insecure we are insecure, and no amount of covering it over will change anything.

Insecurity exists because we wrongly believe we must attain something. Careless thinking declares we must become wealthy or powerful or prominent. Oddly, we seek these goals in an attempt to feel secure, never seeing how the very attempt creates insecurity. How seldom do people pause in their mad scramble to notice this.

Seeking wordly prizes divides you from your real nature. Alienation from your real nature arouses feelings of being in danger. Self-reunion ends insecurity. It is no more complicated than that.

Salt does not spoil because it is its own preservative. Likewise, you become your own protector by living within these principles.

TRUE GOOD

People say they want to know what is truly good for them.

It is good to remember the existence within you of something which can never be discouraged or afraid.

It is good to say, 'I want to know where I am making a fundamental mistake in living my life.'

It is good to see that a right person will not attract wrong circumstances to himself.

It is good to realize that the only valuable rebellion is the rebellion against our own false values.

It is good to know that an inner miracle can happen when our silent receptivity permits it to happen.

It is good to hear, 'Instead of trying to *do* something, try to *see* something.'

TRUST YOUR ABILITY

A woodcutter in early America hung a bell outside his cabin. Shaken by frequent winds, the bell warned the woodcutter against wandering too far into the perilous forest. One day while searching for a particular kind of tree, he carelessly wandered beyond the bell's range. He was lost for three days before finding his way back home.

That is also the story of careless mankind. He forgets, he wanders, he suffers.

But he can come back.

One homeward path is to no longer attribute power where there is no power. As a specific example, do not attribute power to the future. It has no power. Do not believe you will be happier tomorrow. Do not trust next year to deliver pleasanter conditions. Trust only your considerable ability to change what you are at this very moment. That is right understanding and right use of power.

TRUTH'S INVITATION

Truth does not say an individual must approach without his angers and frustrations. If a man is bound by these chains he has no choice but to come with them. Asking a prisoner to behave like a free man is both impossible and hypocritical.

Truth says this to the chained man or woman, 'Come with your very angers and frustrations, but add something else. Add a simple and earnest wish to drop your chains. This wish itself is a new power. By permitting it to enter the action you permit it to become the key to liberation.'

No man who asked insincerely ever received an answer. No man who asked sincerely was ever denied an answer. Truth always knows which of the two attitudes is asking.

Inspiration is the beautiful explosion of understanding that occurs when a truth meets a willingness to receive that truth.

TURN HOMEWARDS

Our aim is to live in the here and now. The ditch between us and this aim is wandering thought. So we must cease our mental meandering and come back home, as did the Prodigal Son.

Turn homewards by thinking of a small action you will be performing a few minutes from now. You may be picking up a pencil or entering another room. State your aim, 'The moment I pick up that pencil — I will be aware of myself doing just that.'

See whether you do!

Most people are surprised at how easily they forget such a simple task of remembering themselves in the here and now. But surprise and dismay are beams of light. They destroy the great illusion from which men suffer — the illusion that they are conscious human beings who know what they are doing. So success or failure with the pencil is not the important point. Awareness of unawareness is what we want. That in itself builds a human being who knows what he is doing, and who therefore always does good to himself and others.

TURNING POINTS

One fascinating feature of the path is to see yourself change before your own eyes. These turning points arrive all by themselves as you do what must be done. Their principal ingredient is a new insight. Here are examples:

Realizing that the struggle to win over other people is both exhausting and vain, you turn to self-conquest.

You become more conscious of having a scattered self, which increases the urge for self-unification.

Knowing that most people are too confused in themselves to offer authentic help, you abandon worthless sources of guidance.

More and more you realize that your environment is not outward, but inward, so that is where you go into action.

You see difficulties as opportunities for self-transformation, instead of as enemies.

UNBLOCKING

A man fell heir to some property near the seashore. He wandered for a while in quiet enjoyment of his land, then decided to stroll down to the ocean. With pleasant anticipation of sighting waves and sands, he followed the downward path. He came to a sudden halt as a tall wall blocked his path. With disappointment he reflected to himself, 'Someone does not want me to trespass on his property. Well, it is his wall. There is nothing I can do.'

Over the days he felt a mounting urge to have direct access to the sea. He made up his mind to locate the owner of the frustrating wall. Checking land records, he identified the wall's owner. He then knew who blocked his path and who could therefore open the way. The wall was on his own property.

We block our own path. We can unblock ourselves.

UNCERTAINTY

Only by passing all the way through uncertainty do we come to final assurance. A woman may think, 'Marriage will confer happiness.' A man reasons, 'Financial success will bring security.'

Both make the same mistake, not realizing it. Their personal certainties are false. Both have taken exciting assumptions as final facts. Sooner or later, each will sadly discover that marriage does not deliver happiness, that money does not provide inner safety.

What must we do? We must have no ideas whatever about

the attraction of happiness and security. We must see the difference between *an assumption about happiness* and *happiness itself*. In other words we must enter uncertainty and remain there, not minding any temporary nervousness it causes. It helps to remember that true happiness resides above all mere ideas about happiness.

So stand on uncertain ground. Remain there. Something immense will happen.

UNCONSCIOUS REACTIONS

A teacher told his class, 'You do not as yet fully understand what it means to be a psychological slave. This will be corrected this evening by discussing a specific instance. The daily reactions of most men and women are mechanical and unconscious. They react according to habits and patterns picked up over the years. It is no different from the response of a machine. Push a certain button and the machine jumps into its usual reaction. It cannot do otherwise. Accuse a man of having a hostile nature and what does he do? He proves it with a hostile denial. Since most people never notice this kind of psychological slavery, they are quite sure it does not include them.'

The teacher paused a moment, then said, 'Everything you have just heard is good news. Please tell me why.'

A student volunteered, 'Because self-questioning is a giant step towards self-freedom.'

UNIQUENESS

Are unawakened men and women really different from each other? Is anyone really unique or outstanding? Not from the only right viewpoint, the viewpoint of Reality. Mr A. thinks he is different from Mr B., while Mr C. is convinced he is different from both A. and B. They are in fact exactly the same, for they share the same neurosis; all live in the same haunted house. They are different only on the surface, only in the particular ways they suffer from themselves.

But there is genuine uniqueness. This is seen and experienced by those who have transcended the false belief in a separate self. Strangely, uniqueness appears at the same time it seems to disappear. This is perfectly understandable. Counterfeit uniqueness, with its vanities and sorrows, goes away as self-knowledge increases. Then, the uniqueness of living within the Whole appears to the individual. Having seen what uniqueness is not, he sees and lives what it is.

UNIVERSAL LAW
When a person chooses to act in a certain way he must shoulder the punishing consequences of that action. The distressed person may insist that another carry or share his burden, but it cannot be done. The individual who insists upon wandering in the desert is the person who must come back. No one can come back for him. People sense the truth of this universal law but try to push it away. They demand immunity from the law of cause and effect. That is like demanding that a dropped rock should fall upwards.

The law of cause and effect cannot be broken, but it can be transcended through self-insight. A man must see how his action arouses a reaction on the same level. Hostility provokes hostility. A wish to take advantage of others will arouse their wish to take advantage in return. End the action and the reaction ends.

UNLIMITED CAPACITIES
There are two things which are unlimited — a man's capacity for self-knowledge and his capacity for self-deception.

A student asked his teacher, 'When will I be different?'

'When you can see the difference between living consciously and living unconsciously while dreaming that you are living consciously.'

'I want to see the difference.'

'How badly do you want it? Everything depends upon that. See the difference and you will live the difference. The seeing is the living itself.'

No one can reach a destination he does not want to reach. No one can understand a truth he does not want to hear.

Anyone can possess that which his deeper nature wants to

possess. Anyone can have everything that is truly valuable.

UNNATURAL RESPONSES

A soldier volunteered to infiltrate several enemy armies as a spy. Since each foreign army had a different kind of salute, he had to strain to remember each one on each occasion. Exposure could result from a wrong salute. So wherever he travelled in enemy country, he trembled with fear at the very thought of a wrong reaction.

Only when returning home did his nervousness end.

That is how most people suffer through their days. Feeling threatened by a foreign land, they acquire unnatural responses which they hope will somehow provide protection. But every challenge is a new tension, for exposure could follow a mistake.

That is not living at all. That is agonizing. And that is why you are adventuring inwardly.

UNNECESSARY THOUGHTS

Become increasingly aware of unnecessary thoughts. Interrupt habitual mental movements as often as possible during the day in order to examine them. The very interruption allows clear judgment of the nature of passing thoughts. It is like getting out of your car in order to inspect faulty parts.

A profound awareness of how unnecessary thoughts subtract from us is enough to end them. If you know the nature of salt water you do not pour it into a fish bowl requiring fresh water. It is good to find our own examples of useless ideas. One person might become conscious of maddening repetitions. Another might see how he is dominated by the desire to be noticed.

Necessary thoughts are those which contribute in some way to psychological health. Keep this in mind, then regularly dismiss all other kinds of thoughts.

UNREAL ROLES

Angry anguish can be traced back to one cause. It is our inability to succeed in our starring roles in our self-built theatre. A man selects the role of being someone who is entitled to money and respect and attractive women. His stage identity is labelled, I AM A PERSON WHO IS OWED MONEY AND RESPECT AND WOMEN. But his role is not real. It is not in accord with universal cosmic action in which there are no individual stars with special rights.

Angry anguish. That is all his performance will ever attract. Universal life simply will not follow the script he tries to force upon it. Equally bad, dozens of other tense actors leap onstage to demand the starring role he has claimed for himself. Even if his performance seems applauded one night, he dreads an empty theatre the next night.

No role, no angry anguish. Neither is necessary.

UNWANTED HABITS

Lewis said, 'I don't understand. You say we must become clearly aware of an unwanted habit. But you also say we must not give attention to a habit, for that strengthens it.'

'You must first make a habit conscious, which means to see clearly how it has captured you. Do that, then give it no more attention. Habits exist on the level of mechanical thought. See this. Next, see that any mechanical thought about a habit, such as worry, keeps the mechanicalness in motion. Break arising mechanical thought by suddenly becoming conscious of yourself, for example, by being aware of where you are. As consciousness replaces mechanicalness, the habit fades and stops. When you don't add fuel to a fire, what happens to the fire?'

UNWISE BUILDERS

There was once a village where carpentry had become a lost skill. The people had neglected home-building for so long they no longer knew how to build safe and comfortable dwellings. Hearing about an expert carpenter, they called him in with the request, 'Please show us how to build adequate homes.' He agreed to build a model home to serve as their example.

After a few days the carpenter noticed a change in the

attitude of the people towards him. Their former humility and co-operation had turned into sarcasm and criticism. It was obvious that they had developed a strange jealousy of his great skill.

Before the model home was half-finished the people's hostility had grown into an aggressive rage. Using threats and insults they ordered the carpenter out of town. Quietly picking up his tools, the carpenter departed.

The next day the excited people began to build homes for themselves. Some gave up in despair after a few hours. Others finished their homes, which collapsed in the first wind.

But the greatest tragedy was that no one ever realized how foolish he had been to not learn from one who knew.

USEFUL LESSON

Requested Diane, 'Give us a useful fact about suffering.'

'All suffering can be attributed to our insistence upon trying to prove that an illusion is a reality.'

'For instance.'

'The illusion that we can hurt others without also hurting ourselves.'

'If we really understood that we would never hurt anyone.'

'You can see it. Picture in your mind a poor and wretched man whose only possession is a tree producing sour apples. Since the sour apples are plentiful, he sells them to his equally poor neighbours. Though disliking sour apples, the neighbours put up with them, for that is all they have to eat. Now look at the owner of that apple tree. *The only food he has is the same sour apples he sells to his neighbours, so he must suffer from the same sourness he gives to them.* Do you know how few human beings on earth really see this?'

Said Diane, 'We want to see it. We want a new apple tree.'

USE NEGATIVE FEELINGS

'As you suggested,' said David, 'I mentally noted the painful feelings that passed through me today. It was surprising to see so many. During a morning incident at work I felt foolish over some remarks I made. In the afternoon I was with a group of people when I suddenly felt rejected by them. You have emphasized that self-knowledge begins with self-observation. I have started with this, but what next?'

'There are many ways to use self-inspection, which will be covered in future classes, but here is a general rule. Use painful feelings for positive results. Be like a skilled violin-maker who carves a beautiful instrument from scrap wood. In other words, do not be negative towards negative emotions, but ask how they can aid self-awakening.'

USE OF MIND

Imagine a man lost in the wilderness with only a horse for a companion. Not knowing the way out, the man distracts himself by teaching the horse all kinds of tricks. The animal is taught to trot round in a circle while carrying a load of stones. It is trained to take a drink of water at a shouted command. The horse becomes quite clever — but the man remains lost because he does not ride the horse out of the wilderness.

Man remains in life-wilderness because he fails to let his mind carry him out. Here are three ways anyone can begin to use his mind for self-rescue:

Please your wish for self-transformation instead of pleasing clever but useless activities.

Please what is right instead of pleasing what is noisy.

Please your original mind instead of pleasing what confused society demands of you.

VALUABLE FACTS

'Please supply a helpful fact we may be missing.'

'There is no such thing as a man and his psychological location. He is his own location. His nature is his location. See what this means? Whoever complains about his psychological location is complaining about himself.'

'At yesterday's class you said that spiritual facts can be misused. What did you mean?'

'Spiritual facts are a burden to those who use them for vanity-building purposes. This happens when someone quotes many spiritual facts to boast about his knowledge. But spiritual facts are a guide to whoever uses them to rise above vanity. This occurs when someone lets a fact destroy a flattering illusion about himself.'

'Esotericism says that negative compulsion activates most human behaviour, which is an obvious fact. But how, then, can we break out to find our true good?'

'Regardless of how it now seems, no one is compelled to act against his true good. Compulsion operates only when we fail to see the alternative, which is natural and spontaneous action.'

VALUABLE SELF-TRANSFORMATION

It is a fact that invisible thoughts reproduce themselves in the visible world. Knowledge of this can bring fast and valuable self-transformation. We know quite well how a camera faithfully reproduces whatever is in line with its inner sight. If pointed at a sparkling sea, it reproduces that sparkling pleasantness. If aimed towards a field of weeds, it reveals the actual condition of that field.

See the same reproductive process at work in your mind. And remember, it is what you really think that duplicates itself in the exterior world, not what you assume you think. You *are* what you *see*. You can see as much new and sparkling pleasantness as you really want to see.

VALUELESS THOUGHTS

Said a teacher to some inquirers, 'If your usual ways of thinking and acting have done nothing for you, why continue with them? May I tell you the two reasons why you cling to useless thoughts? First, you do not know there is another way to think and act. Never having explored the higher regions of your own mind, another way does not exist to you. So from your present viewpoint it seems perfectly logical for you to decline an investigation. Why search, you reason, for something that does not exist. It exists all right, but not for you at present.'

Continued the teacher, 'What I will say next may sound a bit severe, but we are not here to hurt anyone, but to learn. The second reason you cling to valueless thoughts is because you prefer to protect your delusions instead of exposing and ending them. You fear that the new will end the old, but that is precisely what must happen if you are to find yourself.'

VALUES

'What do you consider valuable?' The answer to that question tells a lot about the person answering. Today, listen carefully to what your friends and relatives talk about. You will soon see what they value. Is it really valuable?

There are man-made values and there are cosmic values. The less the man-made, the more the cosmic, so now we know how to become cosmically wealthy. We must recognize and drop human values.

An earnest person can tell the difference between true and false values by asking himself, 'How do I feel towards my own company? Am I at ease with myself or am I nervous? If

I had to depend only upon myself for making my way through this world, could I do it? Would I have a quiet confidence towards success?' These questions are enlightening because a man does not *possess* values, rather, he *is* his values. His entire nature consists of whatever he values at any particular moment. So as values become richer, so does the man, for they are the same thing.

VERIFY FOR YOURSELF

The golden thread of esoteric truth runs through various religions and philosophies. However, it has been covered over by man-made organizations and superstitions. So verify everything for yourself. Suppose you are part of an audience hearing a sermon or lecture. The speaker declares, 'Your mind is a king! Let it rule!' Esoterically, that is true. Each man's mind is indeed a monarch, but unfortunately, most people have abdicated the throne.

However, we have some questions about the speaker himself. Has he established his own mind as a king, or is he merely repeating mechanically a truth he picked up somewhere? Does his private life match his public preaching?

The speaker next urges, 'Go into action! Action is all that counts. Get involved in making this a better world.' This is horrible advice. Any action apart from self-knowledge heads straight for the howling jungle — which today's news reports prove.

The mind which indeed reigns as king knows instantly the difference between sense and nonsense.

VESSEL OF GOLD

During the California gold rush a sailing vessel was due in New York harbour about the first of July. Awaiting its cargo of gold, the ship's owners watched the seas anxiously as July came and passed. At the end of August the ship was given up as lost at sea. But its sails were sighted on the fifth day of September, after which it entered the harbour with its rich cargo. The vessel had not been lost at all. Severe storms had forced it to make several extra stops for repairs.

Every man and woman is a vessel of gold who has not reached the harbour as yet.

See the riches of your true nature. The reason you are never really denied anything is because you can never be denied your own cosmic self.

At the start a man wonders, 'How can this be true?' With the advance of psychic maturity he affirms, 'I see how this is true in a way I never saw before.'

VIBRATIONS

Conquest of your own negative emotions guarantees conquest of the negative states of others. When their frenzied vibrations do not arouse similar vibrations in you, conquest is complete. Instead of having negative reactions to others, you simply see before you frightened and reckless people who know no other way to behave.

See how self-conquest insures other-conquest. Having won over yourself, you do not think about winning over others or about losing to them. Having won the supreme victory within, you are above these opposites. You now see something very clearly. You see that the other man's negative state was never ever your problem; the only difficulty was your own negative response to it. After all, you cannot feel his storm; you can only feel your own.

Cut the invisible rod between you and others, then you will not vibrate to their wrong behaviour.

VICTORY IN DEFEAT

Explorers tried for hundreds of years to find the source of the White Nile by travelling upstream from Egypt. Hostile tribes, papyrus swamps, and the fierce heat of the desert combined to defeat the invasions. Later explorers decided to attack from an entirely new direction which would avoid the usual obstacles. Launching their expedition from the east coast of Africa, they marched inland. The new route led them to the source of the White Nile — Lake Victoria.

To find ourselves we must strike out in an entirely new direction. The usual ways, with their false comfort, must be seen as self-defeating and therefore useless. Defeat of our present ways is the best thing that could happen to us, providing it turns us towards a way we have not considered before.

VIEW OF LIBERTY

Mr and Mrs B. called to have a general discussion. At one point Mr B. stated, 'We feel dominated by fear, but do not know what to do with it.'

'See consciously what you now fear unconsciously. Consciousness and fear cannot exist together. So now you must understand what it means to see something consciously. It starts, as does all liberty, with self-viewing. Look inwards. See something you hesitate to see. For example, you may fear the ending of a certain pleasure at present possessed. You can then go on to view something that millions of human beings never see. You can see why you fear its ending. It is because you wrongly associate the pleasure with your self-identity, that is, you take the feeling as being your actual nature, which it is not. So what you really fear is the ending of yourself. Now the door opens wider. You see that the very ending of false ideas about yourself is what you really want, for it also ends fear.'

VIEWPOINT

An inquirer insisted to a teacher of the path, 'I am right.'
    'From whose viewpoint are you right?'
    'From my own viewpoint.'
    'What if that viewpoint is wrong?'
    'But what if it is right?'
    'Honestly, now, are you content?'
    'No.'
    'Then your viewpoint must be wrong.'
    'How come?'
    'Because your viewpoint determines your feelings.'
    'Perhaps.'
    'On what condition would you change your viewpoint?'
    'On the condition that it delivered contentment.'

'Then what are you waiting for?'

VISITOR
An insincere man wished to make an appointment with a widely honoured teacher of truth. He approached the teacher's assistant with the request, 'Please set down time and place for me to see your superior.'

The assistant, who knew a few things about human nature, nodded. 'First you must pass a test which will reveal your ability or inability to benefit from seeing the teacher. Are you willing to take the test?'

'Yes, yes,' the visitor impatiently agreed.

The assistant nodded once more. 'I see. Please let me ask you a question. Why do you wish to see the teacher?'

'I want his advice.'

'Do you truly want his advice or do you merely wish to be the centre of his attention?'

The visitor replied angrily, 'Of course I want his advice. Let's get on with the test of my sincerity.'

'You just had it.'

VOLUNTEERS
The leader of a class in Toronto, Canada, began the evening by saying, 'This is volunteer night. Volunteer anything informative and helpful to the rest of the class.'

A student said, 'I finally understand a lesson given last month. We were instructed to not be the slave of another person's neurosis. I observed my reactions when others showed hostility towards me. I saw how it scared and subdued me. I am now aware of my slavery, so am off to a good start towards ending it.'

Volunteered a second student, 'I have been studying wrong ideas. False ideas are like counterfeit money which people pretend to value, but which they want to pass off on to someone else. This made me think more deeply about the only source of true ideas — our purified nature. The mind that finds itself never accepts another man's map, but makes its own.'

VOYAGE TO NEWNESS

We must have correct instructions for making the voyage to newness. They can come only from a man who lives from his own mind.

A man who lives from his own mind might ask a troubled inquirer, 'What are you worried about?' But he is more likely to ask, '*Who* are you worried about?' The teacher asks this because he knows exactly where the worrier has gone wrong. His question has the intention of getting the inquirer back on the right road. The troubled person still believes he consists of his accumulated bundle of memories and experiences. By challenging this false identity the teacher leads the worrier towards his own challenge of it. The time will come when the self-investigator sees that worry continues because the false self-picture continues. He then knows what to do, which is to drop the imaginary self, which he does with great relief.

WALK AWAY

Every man or woman who wants to become a different kind of human being should study the following ideas carefully.

There are thousands of distractions and self-deceptions available to mankind. Most people frantically collect all they can get. But all of them combined are not enough to prevent agony and terror from breaking through. No man-made locks and bolts are strong enough to prevent ghosts from invading and haunting the human house. Where has the individual gone wrong? By living in artificiality. Distractions are desperate artificialities. The fear is intense, for a man on a mental vacation always fears the day he must return to work.

To become a different kind of human being a man must begin to walk beyond his favourite distractions. Even from the viewpoint of everyday happiness and efficiency, no other course makes sense.

So dare to walk away from distractions. It is by this method that we find our way back home.

WATCH HUMAN NATURE

At your first opportunity, watch any group of people debating a controversial topic, such as religion or politics. Quietly but alertly sit there and watch human nature express itself — which will be unconscious and mechanical expression. You will be observing human beings dwelling under psychic hypnosis, who believe themselves to be wise and decisive. They are neither. They are scared and confused human beings who have never seen themselves as they really are.

Be sure to remain a neutral observer. Do not take sides. Neither agree nor disagree with anything anyone says. Concentrate on seeing men and women as they exist beneath their habitual masks. Watch faces which suddenly become defensive or hostile or perplexed. Notice that woman in brief distress at being caught out of her usual role of being a pleasant person. See that man playing the role of a superior scholar who is tensely anxious to make others think it is real. Be aware of the arrogance and contempt, the frozen smiles, the pathetic attempts to appear composed.

See people as they really are. It promotes self-transformation.

WATCH WITH INTEREST

What about those times when you feel all alone, having neither exterior supports nor sympathizing thoughts?

Each time you are thrown back on yourself you have a great opportunity to lose the weak parts of your psychic system. So make the most of it. When all alone, with no rescuing friends or comforting plans, be sure to stay all alone. This can be done when surrounded by people, for you are practising psychological aloneness. Standing all alone forces weak thoughts to depart, and invites strong ideas to enter.

So remain alone. Watch with intense interest the different inner condition this creates. This is a conquering condition. The gate is opening. Remain where you are until it opens so wide you see the other land!

WAYS OF APPROACHING TRUTH

Wishing help in expanding his business, the owner of a large store decided to consult a merchandising expert. On his way to the appointment he met a friend. The owner mentioned his appointment, after which the friend asked, 'What is that paper in your hand? Questions to ask?'

'No,' said the owner. 'I have a plan for expanding my business, which I want him to approve.'

'But what, if he rejects it?'

'Then it proves he is no expert.'

Are we approaching truth with an open and teachable mind, or do we merely wish approval of our preferred plan? Are we getting out of our own way, or are we only appearing to do so? Are we desiring that which will transform us, or are we seeking that which will please us?

WEATHER CONDITIONS

There was once a man who loved to roam the woods and fields surrounding his cabin, observing the ways of nature. One stormy season he was forced to remain indoors for most of the time. Visitors said to him, 'It must be hard for you to be denied your customary strolls.'

The man showed them some figures of birds and animals he had carved from wood. 'Regardless of the storm outside,' he replied, 'I always have an enjoyable time.'

The interior man can always have a good time regardless of exterior storms. The inner is independent of the outer. The ups and downs of an incoherent society have no negative effect on the person who knows himself. His creativity is not restricted by seasons or circumstances.

Reader, think what this means: Be your own fair weather.

WHAT ESOTERICISM MEANS

A group of students in France entered the classroom to see the following lesson on the blackboard:

Learn what esotericism means when it says:
One right thought can banish every pain and trouble.
There is a special kind of indifference which wins.
Inquire into your relationship with yourself.
The description of the lake is not the lake itself.
Happiness comes only through self-unity.
Change arising from habitual thought is no change at all.
Be attentive to everything you think and do.
There is a place of silence between two thoughts.
Think of the present moment as your great treasure.
Refuse the false pleasure of fiery feelings.
Do not permit conditioned thought to distort events.
Take your mind beyond its traditional boundaries.

WHAT OTHERS THINK

The attitudes that others have towards us have no power to hurt or influence us. The damage occurs through our incorrect thinking towards their thinking.

One man was disturbed by believing that several friends criticized him behind his back. Whether they actually did or not is beside the point. The only point is his agitated reaction towards his own assumption. His disturbance appeared to throw out a chain which bound him to the others. The others had nothing to do with the chain; it was his own idea.

What he must do, finally, is to simply have no concern with what others think of him. Achievement can come by replacing his fictitious self with his natural self. Nature is blissfully unconcerned.

WHAT TO DO

Wilbur admitted, 'I don't know what to do with myself. Should I move to another city or stay where I am? Should I buy a certain item or do without it? Should I enter a particular human relationship or stay clear? Why is life so difficult?'

'Nothing is difficult once you end the notion that exterior results should match your inner desires. You desire a certain result while wrongly believing it will provide fulfilment or security. So the yearning for this result becomes a false god. You never notice that gaining previous false gods left you just as shaky as ever; it just pushed tension out of sight for a short time. Do not love the thrill of winning what you want and do not love the frustration of losing. Both are false thrills. This is, by the way, the basic problem of compulsive gamblers. Have no concern when results fail to match your desires. You will then know what to do with yourself every second.'

WHAT YOU POSSESS

A business firm hired some efficiency experts to speed up the company's operations. When the plan was finally set in motion a supervisor noticed an employee who ignored it. When questioned about it the employee apologized, 'Sorry, but my work had to be done at once.'

You have a way of doing things which is far superior to anything devised by society. Find it. Here are some clues.

A man can behave from the pressures of external authority or he can act out of his own free and unified nature. The trouble is, few people know the difference in the two. The only ones who know are those living from their own free nature. They are the self-efficient ones.

What do we possess? Whatever we have given ourselves, for happiness or grief. No outside agency can give or take anything. So it is a wise man or woman who inquires, 'Up to now, what have I given myself?'

WHEN NO ONE CARES
Esoteric science knows the real answer. The real answer is the only answer.

Suppose you feel that no one — either human or divine — cares for you. No one cares how you feel and no one cares what happens to you. This is the gnawing fear of almost everyone, admitted or not. You will say this is a terrible agony. Well, it is, but only because you do not see something utterly fantastic. What if you saw that there is no one in existence who needs to be cared for? That is a fact, for no one exists as a labelled self who needs someone to care for him. There is no you *and* comfort, no you *and* God. There is no self apart from the Whole. See this and the whole agony of wanting someone to care for you collapses.

You should know that very few human beings ever travel this far into the world of fantastic perception. But you can enter it.

WHERE TRUE WISDOM STARTS
What are you trying to change? A troublesome condition in the home? Another person's attitude towards you? A problem connected with sex?

Never try to change anything except the way you think. That is the entire solution, so stick with it from now on. If you wander from it, come back again and again. Never mind if the idea is not clear to you as yet. The very awareness of your uncertainty is the start of true wisdom. Blocked by vanity, the majority of human beings do not know that they do not know. But you are successfully breaking through the trapdoor over your head. You understand that you do not understand. Stay on that course. Find other places where you misunderstand. Your awareness of them is a special kind of light. That light changes the way you think, after which you will understand, after which you will be a different kind of human being.

WHERE VIRTUE EXISTS

When you are about to speak to someone about finances or dinner or gardening, you should use memory to prepare your conversation in advance. The amount of thought given to it depends upon the importance of the matter.

But when you are about to speak to someone about God and goodness and truth, you should prepare nothing at all. Here is why. Memory rightly serves us when handling the everyday matters of finances and dinner. Wishing to know how to cash a cheque today we remember how we cashed one yesterday. That is right use of memory.

But God and goodness do not exist in memory. Memory is mechanical, so any so-called goodness we draw from it will have a mechanical nature, having no real life, no power to guide and heal. Virtue does not exist in memory-time; it exists only in the Pure Present.

So when speaking about spiritual subjects, leave memory out of it. Speak only from the Pure Present. That is where God and goodness exist.

WHISPER OF GOOD

While reading a book you have probably had a certain experience. All of a sudden you feel the urge to stop reading. At first you are not sure of what is happening, then comes a whisper from your mind, 'Wait. Go back. Note that misspelled word.' Your knowledge of right spelling caught an error. You feel better only after observing the mistake and correcting it in your mind.

It is our faculty of psychological correction which must be heeded and obeyed. It whispers for our good. We must not be upset over any interruption it makes in our day, for that is part of the correction. Knowing what is right, this faculty requires only our co-operation in order to make us right.

It is the way of delight to let new understanding shine upon difficulties to make them disappear, just as dew disappears under sunlight.

WHOLE MIND

Most human beings are fixed on the level of mechanical thinking. They think what they think because that is what they always think. This produces many familiar figures you see in the world of people. It includes the so-called intellectual who preaches dramatically — and endlessly — but who is merely a parrot who repeats what he has heard from another parrot.

One of our aims is to go beyond mechanical thinking to a full use of the mind. Only a whole mind knows compassion, for it has put an end to the artificial compassion of the mechanical mind.

To rise above habitual thought, take paper and pencil. Write down any sentence from this book which appeals to you. Read and reflect until its meaning is clear in your mind. Next, write down its meaning in your own words and in a single sentence. Just let yourself go and express the same thought in any way you like. Do this with other sentences. It makes *a* thought *your* thought. Instead of merely describing a sparkling stream, you personally swim in that stream!

WHOLE WORLD

Any time you fearfully feel the world is closing in on you, stop that feeling at once. Replace it with awareness of a fact. The fact is, the world cannot close in on you because there is no world *and* you at all. You are not apart from the Whole World; you and the Whole World are the same thing. So do not think from that part of the mind which divides everything into opposites, such as you and I, you and success, you and the world. Think from your whole mind and the illusion of separation vanishes. In this new thinking you can never feel that the world is closing in on you.

Take this opportunity to turn mental insights into practical actions. Apply the ideas you have just read to daily life. For instance, see that feelings of financial pressure exist in you, not in the outer world. Now, where must you regain self-command through self-insight? Within.

WILLINGNESS

In class one evening, Mr and Mrs J. spoke about their progress. Mr J. began, 'Here is something we have learned about ourselves and others. A person's unwillingness to listen to what he must hear will be equalled by his distress. The unhappier the person, the less will he listen to what could save him. His very anxiety refuses the medicine. A man might have the surface appearance of being interested in the rescuing facts, but his secret negativities have no intention of being dismissed from their dark thrones.'

Mrs J. continued, 'All this can be restated from the positive viewpoint. A person's cosmic health will occupy the same level as his willingness to listen to facts which upset his cherished but mistaken ways. So there is just one kind of individual who really goes places. He is the one who is as open to esotericism as the shore is open to the sea.'

WIN GREATER SELF-RELIANCE

Commented a member of a study group, 'One fact about society is quite clear to me. It cannot really change or uplift anything. It is captured by self-deception, like a flock of sheep solemnly teaching each other how to fly like birds. To *do* we must *be*.'

When seeking guidance in daily difficulties, do you ever ask why you consult this or that authority?

A man had a broken clock which he wanted repaired. A friend directed him to someone having a reputation as an expert repairman. Later, the two friends met again.

'Did you get him to repair your clock?' came the question.
'No.'

'Why not?'

'I noticed his own clock on the wall. It told the wrong time.'

Remind yourself often of the power of self-reliance. We claim the apples by working in our own orchard. Self-reliance increases with self-knowledge.

WINNING WORDS

Words and phrases can express victorious attitudes. Make the following twelve winners your own:

'From now on I will work for my true interests.'

'Walking in circles is not for me.'

'I will hear what parts of me do not want to hear.'

'Something needs correction.'

'I will not argue with what is true and right.'

'No more borrowed beliefs!'

'I intend to go all the way.'

'Psychological storms, rightly used, teach wisdom.'

'I have been asleep long enough.'

'Every new second is a new start.'

'Even though timid, I will take the leap.'

'Tell me more!'

WISE CAPTAIN

Imagine a small boat adrift in a vast sea. Huddled in it are several survivors of a shipwreck. Quite naturally, all of them are eager to reach the safety of shore. However, only one of them really knows how to navigate the boat towards land. He offers to take charge of the rescue voyage, but the others shove him aside with nervous arguments. One by one the others try to steer the boat, but everyone senses they are drifting in circles. All the while the knowledgeable man patiently speaks about his qualifications as a skilled seaman. The others calm down long enough to see how wisely he talks about winds and currents and directions. Convinced of his skill, they appoint him their captain. When finally sighting land, they are glad they did.

Man is a rocking boat crowded with argumentative and self-glorifying personalities. But there is also one wise and calm self which knows how to do the good and necessary. So listen for him, listen to him, and appoint him the captain.

WONDERS OF NATURE

Henri Frederic Amiel was a philosopher and a lover of nature. His fragile health confined him to the regions around his mountainous home in Switzerland. Like Henry David Thoreau, Amiel delighted in strolling among the beauties of the unspoiled land. One typical pleasure came when he was *'lying under a tree and visited by three butterflies.'*

Amiel was fascinated constantly at the natural wonders encountered on his walks. He writes, *'I went out into the garden to see what progress the spring was making. Delightful surprise!'* He had discovered a small plant that had flowered during the night.

While strolling, Amiel was also pondering. He reflected, *'We must know how to put occupation aside, which does not mean that we must be idle. In an inaction which is meditative and attentive . . . the soul itself spreads, unfolds, and springs afresh, and, like the trodden grass of the roadside . . . becomes new, spontaneous, true and original.'*

WORLD CONQUEST

If your usual ways of handling your world have not worked, try this one.

Do not strain to hold your world in place. That is a tiring and unnecessary task. Let your world be whatever it wants to be, after which you will be who you really want to be. Why is this so? Because your undivided nature will realize that you and your world are One, and that it was always this way in reality. You conquer the world by *being* the world. Reflect on this every day.

Many people cannot accept anything that cannot be seen or heard. This limited thinking prevents entrance into the invisible world of higher power. The science of mathematics cannot be seen, yet it can be used for practical purposes. Esoteric science is like that.

WORLDWIDE CHAOS

'Please comment on social rebellion.'

'A man's rebellion against anything except his own misunderstanding will only perpetuate the world's confusion. Social chaos is the sum of thousands of individual confusions. But how many people will allow this obvious fact to penetrate?'

'What can be done about it?'

'Individual and collective healing will start when self-evasion and self-deception end. Everyone offers to help a screaming society, everyone claims to have the answers. Everyone lowers his bucket but never asks what is in the well.'

'Where does an enlightened man fit into the picture?'

'An awakened man knows what he is doing, but few others can follow and understand his actions. His secret ways no more exist to the hypnotized man or woman than a diamond exists to a sheep. Just try to tell a sheep about a diamond. However, human beings who are tired of being sheep can be told about higher actions.'

WORTHWHILE FRIENDSHIP

Asked Stuart, 'Christ and others taught that we should be in the world, but not of it. What does that mean?'

'It means you can have social and physical relationships with others while having nothing to do with them spiritually and psychologically. Light and darkness cannot mix. But beware of self-deception here. Someone can easily imagine he is spiritual and noble, yet be a major contributor to human madness. You will be in the world but not of it when you no longer think others owe you something.'

Dorothy contributed, 'This indicates a need to look closely at what society calls friendship.'

'Authentic and worthwhile friendship occurs when something true in you communicates with something true in another person. All else is dependency, self-interest, artificial behaviour, or some other counterfeit of authentic friendship.'

XENOCRATES
In modern language, the ancient Greek philosopher Xeno-
crates said something like this: 'You have a philosophy of
life? All right. Let's see what it does for you. Let's see how it
influences your daily conduct. Does it make you a good and
a pleasant human being? Does it keep you calm in a crisis?
Does it provide accurate guidance and effortless action? Test
your philosophy in everyday affairs. Honestly, now, how
much is it worth?'

This frank talk has considerable value, for it refuses to go
along with self-deception and compromise. It enables a man
to make a decision. The wise man decides in favour of
himself, not in favour of wordy philosophies.

When do we have a true philosophy? When there is no
difference between the philosophy and the philosopher.

XEROPHYTE
A xerophyte is any kind of plant which carefully conserves
the water it receives. This talent for not wasting water
enables it to thrive in deserts. Sagebrush and cacti are
examples.

Be like that plant. Conserve your psychic energy. Do not
waste it in daydreams or in pointless social involvements. The
first step is to be aware of wastage, so make this your aim for
today. Detect and abolish anything that drains your natural
powers. Many beginners in esotericism start with their speech
habits. For instance, they slow down and eventually abolish
idle chatter.

Place your energies on the side of self-awakening. Economy in using inner powers is one sign of a truly wise mind. Whatever is not wasted in frivolous activities can be used for attaining the Great Aim. This should be a very thrilling thought to those who cherish the Great Aim.

X-RAYS

The value of X-rays is in their power to penetrate solid matter and reveal hidden conditions. Likewise, esotericism provides power to see through external appearances to understand what really happens in human affairs. With psychic X-rays we see through ourselves and others, thus opening a new world worthy of conquest.

Take a person who wants to be involved in society but wishes to avoid getting hurt by it. That is like wanting to be a lion tamer but demanding that lions behave like doves.

We must get out of the social cage altogether, not by retreat, but by seeing through society's false ways. That leads us to the new world of worthwhile conquest — self-conquest.

At the end of each day ask yourself, 'What did I work for today — the temporary or the lasting?'

XYLOPHONE

Like a xylophone, a man's nature sends out harmony or discord, according to the accuracy of the musician.

The only thing on earth that really persecutes a man is his own unconscious wrongness.

Anyone feeling he is out of step with the world should question whether it is worthwhile to be in step with the world.

People fear that truth wishes to force them inside a fence, which is a very common fear among people living inside a fence.

Knowing what one wants is not the same as knowing the difference between right and wrong.

To begin to see the answer a man must expose his hidden fear that there might not be an answer.

The needle of truth can be found in the haystack of

falsehood only when one has made an effort to learn what a needle looks like.

A sincere person hearing truths which upset him should be exceedingly eager to hear the next upsetting truths.

YEARNING FOR KNOWLEDGE

A woman in class introduced herself as a visitor from New Zealand. She then asked, 'What would it be like to meet a teacher who really understands the mysteries of life?'

'If you ever meet a man who really knows, he knows ten-thousand times more than you think he knows. However, there is no way for you to know this at present, for anything above your present level of perception does not exist for you. This explains why some people scorn or distort that which they cannot understand. You can't talk to a sparrow about stars. Let this information aid your advancement. Resolve to never reject an idea just because it fails to agree with what you already accept as true.'

The visitor nodded in agreement. 'Earlier this evening someone stated that a teacher can teach only the teachable. That is certainly true. I want to increase my yearning for knowledge.'

YEAR OF PROGRESS

Two students of esotericism volunteered to report on their progress over the year.

One student stood up to say, 'I used to suffer deeply from feeling misunderstood. It seemed that no one could enter my world with sympathy and understanding. It was hard to face at first, but this was a classic case of self-centredness. I finally realized what it meant to be a prisoner of one's own error. At one of the meetings, someone made a particularly helpful remark. He said that every prisoner unconsciously consents to his chains. I have withdrawn my consent.'

The other student reported, 'I used to go around doing what I thought was good works. I tried to live up to a flattering self-picture of being a friendly and helpful person. All the time I was a smouldering volcano, ready to explode. There was deep resentment of the role I thought I had to play. Of course I tried to hide my hostility from others in order to keep my public image intact. Only these teachings save me from — from I don't know what kind of disaster. I was shown how to see myself as I really was, while not being frightened or ashamed. That was the start that led to liberty from my terrible self-conflict and self-punishment.'

YELLOW DOVE

A husband and wife lived in a woodland cottage at the base of a mountain. One morning the wife found an injured dove on the ground. While caring for it they inspected its unusually brilliant golden-yellow feathers. They agreed they had never before seen a bird like this in the surrounding trees.

The dove slowly recovered, but seemed restless and unhappy. The puzzled wife experimented by feeding it different kinds of foods, but the bird remained as despondent as before.

Intrigued by the mystery, the wife secured a book about birds. After a while she explained the solved mystery to her husband. 'It is not native to this area,' she said. 'It belongs on the other side of the mountain. An unusual storm must have carried it away from its natural habitat.'

The yellow dove was taken to the other side of the mountain. When released it sang cheerfully and flew away. Commented the wife, 'Now we understand. It just wanted to go home.'

The husband philosophized, 'Like man.'

YES AND NO

Ask yourself, 'From higher spiritual altitudes, what does it mean to learn from hurtful experiences?' The answer is fascinating. It can be more easily understood by seeing what it means to not learn from experience. We refuse the lesson in disappointments and frustrations because we do not see them as the very healing medicines we need. We wrongly take 'no' as a threat to our existence, which then cuts us off from the medicines. What is frustration? It is nothing more than a blockage to a man's insistence that his personal desires should rule the world. When this unconscious demand is refused by reality, the man feels defeated and afraid.

So how does a wise mind use experiences of frustration? He allows them to break down and destroy his false assumption that his survival depends upon a 'yes' to his demands. He must realize that his real nature is above both 'yes' and 'no', therefore, above both frustration and anxiety.

YESTERDAY AND TOMORROW

Mr and Mrs H. usually occupied the same chairs during class. Close to the front, they were in a good position to exchange ideas with the teacher. Mrs H. said one evening, 'Friends sometimes ask what our classes are all about. Although I know quite well why we are here, I find it difficult to explain to them. Sometimes I just say that we wish to straighten out our lives, but I know how vague that sounds to people.'

'We realize,' added Mr H., 'that most people will not understand any more than my wife and I would have understood a few years ago. We are convinced it is best to just drop a single idea into their minds to see whether they are interested in hearing more. This obeys the esoteric rule that these truths must be given only to those who show definite interest. But what is a good way to test sincerity? What might we reply when asked what the class is all about?'

'Tell them it is all about a way to prevent yesterday from becoming tomorrow.'

YIELD TO TRUTH

A member of a class in Colorado commented, 'I fought against it for years, but I now yield to plain logic. Our usual ways of solving social problems only make them worse. Social reformers want to change living conditions, but so does a hurricane. We all think that someone else knows more than we do and can therefore help us. That is abandonment of self-intelligence. More and more I am convinced that no man is better qualified to think for me than myself.'

Agreed a second student, 'I know exactly what Carl is talking about. I also fought fiercely against any idea that did not agree with what I preferred to believe. Truth could no more penetrate my mind than a rock can absorb perfume. It took a severe personal crisis to jolt me out of my arrogant daydream. I will tell you what helped me most of all when I started this class. I was told to not be afraid to drop all ideas which gave me a sense of security. This helped me to see that my security was artificial, so I had everything to gain by losing false ideas based on social imitation. Like Carl, I want to think for myself.'

YOU AND ALONENESS

People are so fearful of being left alone, whether physically, socially, psychologically. They get uneasy when having only their own company. And that is a perfect example of lack of insight. Being alone is an opportunity for standing on your own. Away from those who demand your time and attention you can locate the new power which is never afraid of being alone.

One certain benefit of this is the end of a common torment — the torment of feeling oneself at the mercy of other people. The wife feels at the mercy of her husband's decision to remain or leave her. The businessman feels himself the slave of the rude customer.

Do not be at the mercy of yourself and you cannot be at the mercy of others. Throw away one end of the stick and you also lose the other end. Perhaps the idea of being at the mercy of yourself is new to you. Think about it. Think rightly until the realization dawns that you are not at the mercy of husband or customer or anyone else.

YOU AND WHOLENESS

The person who blazes his own trail has one supreme

advantage. He need not pay for the mistakes of others. Blaze your own trail with the following principles.

The world can be embraced, but it cannot be used. We can try to use the world for what we think are personal benefits, but we must remember the outcome. The personal must be the partial, the limited, the divided. In these states we feel separated, unloved, insecure.

Those who persist along the path will some day end all attempts to use anyone or anything. This happens because they are no longer controlled by the mechanical forces which used to rush them towards supposed advantages which ended in conflict. Such people know what it means to be whole, unlimited, unified.

YOUR ORIGINAL NATURE

A band of refugees fleeing from a land of oppression climbed to the heights of a green mountain. There they discovered a stream with water of great purity and clearness. Climbing even higher they discovered the source of the stream. Wishing to protect its purity, they built a spacious temple over the source of the stream in a way which did not interfere with its flow. So over the years the stream remained a source of refreshment for those who protected its purity.

The source of purity is your own original nature. Discover and protect it. Let no one interfere with its natural flow.

This story was heard in class by Floyd, an airline pilot. He commented, 'That is an excellent illustration of what we must do. I will remember it. However, I always return to the same question. Where can we start the self-exploration which leads us back to our original nature?'

'Your mind works in various ways. Discover whether those ways are beneficial.'

YOUR PURPOSE

Descartes had an interesting method for determining whether scholars with great reputations for wisdom actually possessed what they professed. Descartes selected a truth of which he himself was the master, then presented it to a scholar who called on him. Usually, the scholar appeared to understand the idea also, but at that point Descartes made his test. The scholar was asked to repeat the idea back to Descartes. In most cases the idea was completely distorted from its original form, which proved that it was not really understood.

Investigate everything for yourself. Take no one's word for anything. When anyone tries to teach you something about God or spirituality, ask yourself, 'Is this person speaking from himself or is he merely repeating what he has picked up somewhere?' Anyone with alert mind and eyes can detect the difference. Your purpose is to go beyond recorded mental tapes of what life is all about to a personal experience which sets you free.

YOUTHFUL MIND

There is only one reason why an individual's mind works against him instead of serving him naturally and effortlessly. It is because the person has not explored his own mind long enough to understand its incorrect operation. Suppose a man feels depressed because he is not what society calls a 'success'. He must realize that his conditioned mind has taken a mere word, a mere label, as a reality. Correction comes by realizing that the only worthwhile success is to be an enlightened human being who lives above glittering but worthless human labels.

'Who am I?' is the haunting question in everyone's mind. Reality replies, 'You will never discover who you are by thinking about who you are, for your real nature resides above habitual thought. Only when frantic thought ceases will you know, and it will be totally different than expected.'

A mind which understands this secret is a youthful mind.

ZEAL FOR FACTS

You do not need to get involved in mysterious doctrines or complicated ceremonies. You just need a zeal for facts. Unfortunately, many people prefer mystery and magic because it appears more exciting than facts. This is a dreadful error. It is like preferring a sparkling pebble over an uncut diamond. It is perfectly possible to live without wearing yourself out in futile battles with people and events. What fact is more exciting than that? Every weight upon your mind can be lifted immediately and for ever. Try to equal the excitement of that fact. There are some people in this world who know these facts by personal experience. Join them.

When these ideas were discussed in a class in Iowa, someone commented, 'Assumptions often masquerade as facts. How can we tell one from the other?'

'A fact never leaves you regretting that you chose it. Study past experiences and you will see the difference.'

ZEN

A teacher of Zen invited questions from his class. A student asked, 'What future rewards can be expected by those who strive diligently with their lessons?'

Answered the teacher, 'Ask a question close to home.'

A second student wanted to know, 'How can I prevent my past follies from rising up to accuse me?'

The Zen master repeated, 'Ask a question close to home.'

A third student raised his hand to state, 'Sir, we do not understand. What is meant by asking a question close to home?'

'To see far, first see near. Be mindful of the present moment, for it contains answers about future and past. What thought just crossed your mind? Are you now sitting before me with a relaxed or with a tense physical body? Do I now have your full or partial attention? Come close to home by asking questions such as these. Close questions lead to distant answers.'

ZENITH OF INTELLIGENCE

Remember, there is practical-thinking-towards-daily-affairs and there is awareness-of-yourself-in-action. See the difference in the two ways. When necessary to think about your business or about driving your car, give full attention to these tasks. But when not occupied in particular, as when walking somewhere, be aware of yourself doing whatever you are doing. In time you will be able to switch casually from one way of using your mind to the other way, just as you easily alternate between using left hand and right.

Practical-thinking-towards-daily-affairs and awareness-of-yourself-in-action alternate naturally in the mind which operates wholly. When one is active, the other is passive. The whole mind is working all the time, but in different ways, just as left and right hands express movements of the whole body.

It is the zenith of intelligence to remain within practical-thinking-towards-daily-affairs and awareness-of-yourself-in-action.

ZEPHYR OF REFRESHMENT

'You would think everyone would eagerly welcome these guides.'

'It is a distracted world. People are so distracted by the rough bumps along their psychic detours they can't hear the good news about the open highway ready for instant use.'

'We are now more aware of the falsity of society's standards of success. How might esotericism define success?'

'When hearing a fact about yourself you do not want to hear, and you do not run away, you are a success.'

'Please give us some knowledge about ourselves.'

'An external event does not cause a personal crisis, rather, it reveals the crisis already within. Man is a slumbering crisis, like a ticking time-bomb.'

'I am invigorated by small feelings of rightness which pass through me with increasing frequency.'

'Truth is like a refreshing zephyr blowing across a desert trail leading to the mountains. Any traveller on that trail will feel the zephyr's invigoration.'

ZEST FOR LIFE

Why do we get what we do from life? We receive according to a definite cosmic law. We get what we actually value, not what we say or think we value. Our psychological nature seeks people and events which are like itself. Like attracts like. To change what we get we must change what we value. To change what we value we must get so weary of the futile chase for artificial values that we refuse to run any more.

There can be no zest for life in a man who demands that people and events obey his personal desires. He can have only a counterfeit enthusiasm, like a dinner guest who pretends to enjoy tasteless food. A real zest for life is possessed by whoever is no longer burdened by mechanical demands.

ZIGZAG THINKING

We express our level of understanding or misunderstanding in everything we think and say and do. So it is essential to study the results of any actions we put into motion. The quality or nonquality of results can reveal where an uplifting of causes is necessary. A cause must always produce a similar effect. For a higher effect, put a higher cause into motion.

There is a reason for a zigzagging life. It is zigzagging thinking. Nothing else. Our aim is to end zigzag thinking and go right to the point of discarding the old and obtaining the new.

To be a different person who acts in a different way! That is what we seek. A teacher asked a member of a class, 'Do you know why you are here?'

'Why?'

'So that everything will not continue the way it is.'

ZONES OF INFLUENCE

Human thoughts and human acts have established dozens of zones of influence. There is the influence of the family circle, of office and factory. Men influence and are influenced by politics, churches, social customs. Individuals influenced by these zones can only suffer from them. They always exert degrees of pressure towards mindless obedience and conformity. In many cases the pressure of one zone may push in the opposite direction of another zone, leaving battered and bewildered victims. Sometimes the stunned individual firmly believes he has found security in Zone A, only to be carried off in a mixture of hope and despair by Zones B and C and D.

Do not live like that. Be free of zones. The way to do this becomes clear as you grasp the principle of Oneness. There are no zones in an individual's One Mind which knows itself to be an expression of the Universal One Mind. Instead of noisy zones of influence, there is quiet completeness.

ZOOM UPWARDS

A ground squirrel was seeking food in a meadow when he met a tree squirrel who was also searching around. Deciding to rest for a while, they fell into a discussion of philosophy. The ground squirrel confessed, 'I have tried to find a better life for myself, but have not succeeded. It seems that the world consists only of hard ground and limited supplies.'

Looking at his companion with surprise, the tree squirrel said, 'I am puzzled that you see life like that. My world is vast and abundant.'

'But how can that be?' inquired the ground squirrel.

The tree squirrel suddenly nodded and said, 'I think I understand why you see things as you do. If you would like to view a new world, please follow me up this tree.'

This is the perfect story for any man or woman who wishes to zoom upwards in life.

Praises for
VERNON HOWARD

"Vernon Howard is one of the outstanding teachers of our time, putting you in touch with the secrets of the ages—secrets long buried in the consciousness of man, waiting to be revealed to those with open minds and hearts."
—Dr. David M. Seifert, Ed.D., ABPP

"I know of no one in life or literature who compares to Vernon Howard in enlightened understanding of human problems and solutions."
—Dr. Bruce Tracy, Ph.D

"I had never dreamed that anything so simple could be so absolutely magnificent in showing man about his true nature, the true nature of people and the world."
—Ruth Rand, Executive Secretary

"I have found Vernon Howard's books to be a powerful beam of light in the darkness and confusion surrounding us all in this world."
—Dr. George Collins, DDS